USING POWER AND DIPLOMACY TO DEAL WITH ROGUE STATES

Thomas H. Henriksen

Hoover Institution on War, Revolution and Peace
Stanford University
1999

The Hoover Institution on War, Revolution and Peace, founded
at Stanford University in 1919 by President Herbert Hoover,
is an interdisciplinary research center for advanced study on
domestic and international affairs in the twentieth century.
The views expressed in its publications are entirely those of
the authors and do not necessarily reflect the views of the staff,
officers, or Board of Overseers of the Hoover Institution.

http://www-hoover.stanford.edu

Essays in Public Policy No. 94

Copyright © 1999 by the Board of Trustees of the
   Leland Stanford Junior University

Material contained in this essay may be quoted with appropriate citation.

First printing, 1999

Manufactured in the United States of America
03 02 01 00 99   9 8 7 6 5 4 3 2 1

ISBN 0-8179-5992-0

Library of Congress Cataloging-in-Publication Data
(*not available at time of publication*)

Executive Summary

The end of the cold war a decade ago has ushered in a greatly transformed international landscape. Instead of a pacific era of peace and political harmony, the world, and particularly the United States, has been confronted with a menacing challenge of rogue regimes whose propensity for violence is matched by their intentions to disrupt regional stability, contribute to outlaw behavior worldwide, or to possess weapons of mass destruction. Ruthless rogues also endanger American interests and citizens by their active or passive sponsorship of terrorism. If left unchecked, rogue states such as Iraq, North Korea, Iran, Libya, and others will threaten innocent populations, undermine international norms, and spawn other pariah regimes as the global order becomes tolerant of this political malignancy.

As a major beneficiary of a global order of free markets, free trade, growing prosperity, and spreading democracy, the United States, the world's sole superpower, must take the lead in confronting rogue governments, even though our allies may balk from time to time. Specifically, American power should be used to enhance the credibility of our diplomacy. Law and diplomacy alone are unlikely to affect rogue dictators. They must be reinforced with power. Four broad policy options, which in most cases should be combined rather than implemented individually, can be applied:

- Sanctions and isolation to achieve containment of and inflict economic damage on a rogue state

- International courts and domestic prosecution to bring rogue criminals to justice

- Shows of strength and armed interventions to coerce or eliminate rogue regimes

- Support for opposition movements or covert operations to oust rogue figures

Unless the United States addresses the challenge of rogue states with a combination of force and diplomacy, the new millennium will witness a widening of global anarchy, deteriorating progress toward economic development, and declining political reform. Dire consequences await the United States if it fails to react forcefully to international roguery.

The comments of my colleagues Charlie Hill, James Noyes, Henry Rowen, and Abraham Sofaer were helpful and are gratefully acknowledged along with those from Addison Davis, David Gillette, Bradley Murphy, Douglas Neumann, Piers Turner, and Robin Wright.

USING POWER AND DIPLOMACY TO DEAL WITH ROGUE STATES

"Power and diplomacy work *together*."
—George Shultz[1]

A decade has passed since the toppling of the Berlin Wall spawned a world far different from the cold war order. This new epoch is a treacherous morass characterized by neither peace nor war nor the certitudes of the preceding four decades. Rogue states are derailing our hoped-for political harmony. In the previous era, two superpowers competed politically, economically, militarily, and ideologically across a worldwide landscape. Massive military force, which both sides built up, formed the backdrop to relations between Washington and Moscow. But the sheer destructive power possessed by each contender acted as a brake on risky policies or perilous actions. They restrained their dealings with each other out of the logic of mutual deterrence and self-preservation.

The new global order initially promised peaceful relationships based on market economics, free trade, instantaneous telecommunications, and the liberal movement of financial capital across national borders. These factors would, in turn, lead to the inexorable spread of prosperity and democracy. Politicians and pundits spoke confidently of a new international environment where economic strength counted for more than armaments. Indeed, some commentators held armed forces as passé. Military spending could be drastically cut and the funds directed to ameliorating nations' manifest societal ills. Economic growth would automatically induce less-developed nations to accommodate themselves to the prevailing global model.

But what has become painfully clear during the 1990s is that a handful of rogue states have rejected the global economic order and international standards for their own belligerent practices. Rogue players are less politically encumbered since Soviet Russia (which sponsored anti-American terrorism through surrogates) is no longer exercising a loose restraint over its clients. The United States has also disengaged from credible actions abroad. Rogues confront a global renaissance of spreading democracy and peace with an atavistic challenge that has yet to be met satisfactorily. Superweapons will expand their ambitions, give them deadly bargaining chips, and imperil thousands of innocent lives. Their links to free-wheeling terrorist cells blur the line between state and nonstate actors, complicating standard countermeasures to hold guilty governments accountable.

Meaningful statecraft hinges on power as well as wise policy. Now that the global financial crisis has crippled the belief that economic development alone would guarantee a democratic and peaceful world, America's continued global primacy rests on how it handles renegade states. In the absence of U.S. leadership, anarchy will grow, paving the way for still greater disorder and extremists on the world scene.

This essay explores some policies for dealing with those states that pose the greatest immediate threat. Terrorist rogues throw up deadly challenges to the United States. But we can call on ample examples of past actions for guidance. Lessons can be gleaned from encounters with Iraq, North Korea, Serbia, Iran, Libya, and Cuba over the past few decades. Although history does not set down hard-and-fast principles on statecraft, it does offer analogies and perspective. Tough remedies short of war, in combination, can advance American interests.

The Emergence of Rogue States as Serious Threats

Rogue regimes have always existed in some form or other throughout history. What has changed is the seriousness of their potential threat in the new international disorder. The United States in its earliest days, as one illustration, had to face assaults by the Barbary Coast powers who held U.S. shipping hostage for ransom. James Madison freed American commerce in the Mediterranean from the degrading practice of paying tribute by dispatching sufficient naval forces there.

The cold war also witnessed pariah states, forerunners to today's rogue nations. Because of their extreme diplomatic isolation, questions of their legitimacy, and international opprobrium, these pariahs looked to their own defense, striving to obtain nuclear weapons. In the late 1970s, South Africa, Taiwan, Israel, and South Korea felt their strategic vulnerability and moved to acquire nuclear bombs to redress their weakness. Pressed hard by Washington, Taiwan, South Africa, and South Korea came off the atomic pariah listing when they ceased pursuing their own nuclear weapons agendas. Other states that met some of the standards of a pariah in the previous era included Rhodesia, Chile, Uganda, and Cuba. But with changing circumstances, they also slipped from this categorization, with the exception of Cuba.[2]

Contemporary rogue states, like some of their cold war predecessors, receive diplomatic backing from major power patrons. China and Russia sell advanced technology and weapons to Iraq and Iran. Sudan, in turn, receives financing from Iran for terrorist activities. Serbia gets Russian support. The major players have their own ends in mind. Russia makes common cause with Iran, for example, to offset Turkish gains in Central Asia and to garner hard currency for its technology exports. France has commercial interests in mind when it bucks U.S. resolutions on Iraq in the United Nations. So while being largely independent actors, rogue states can still serve the agenda of greater powers.

Unlike the cold war era, however, rogue regimes are now more technologically independent of the major powers as well as politically freer. A diffusion of scientists and engineers means that advanced industrial states no longer have exclusive capabilities in advanced weapons systems. Third world regimes now have access to expertise from their own Western-trained scientists or from expatriates who have left post-Soviet Russia in search of jobs. They also can readily attain the equipment and materials needed to manufacture weapons of mass destruction and missiles. Iran's advances in mid- and long-range missiles and Iraq's strides in developing nuclear, chemical, and biological capabilities bear witness to the changed global circumstances. Likewise, North Korea, one of the world's poorest and most isolated nations, possesses both nuclear and missile capabilities that threaten its neighbors. Pyongyang raised apprehensions afresh in the summer of 1998 with its three-stage rocket launch over Japan to put a satellite into orbit.

Not all ruthless regimes pose a danger to Americans or to U.S. interests, however. There are, in fact, gradations of bad behavior. One group could be dubbed *diplomatic* outcasts. This designation arises from these states' flouting international norms, making them unwelcome diplomatically in the world community. They are known for their human rights abuses, repressive governments, and lack of political reform. But they do not endanger their neighbors or threaten regional stability. Such states include Cambodia, Myanmar (formerly Burma), Belarus, Nigeria, and Kenya. Others pursue foreign policies that inflict damage on neighbors and thwart crucial U.S. initiatives. Rwanda and Uganda fall into this category because of their military invasion supporting Congolese Tutsi insurgents against the central Congo government.

A second category of troublesome nations has developed from *failed states*. With a relaxation of the East-West tensions, the phenomenon of intrastate anarchy captured international attention. Marked by civil war, political anarchy, and the breakdown of civil authority, the states of Somalia, Sierra Leone, Liberia, Haiti, and Rwanda fragmented or plunged into mass slaughter. Each of these failed states required some form of international intervention to alleviate human suffering. Yugoslavia shared a similar downward spiral, but its breakdown acted as a vortex, dragging in neighboring states and dissolving Balkan stability.

A few pundits have characterized India and Pakistan as *democratic rogues* for going ahead with nuclear tests in May 1998 in the face of international opposition. This mislabeling corrupts the understanding of the already vague term *rogue*, which, in the case of India and Pakistan, has been misapplied to states exercising assertive defense options. Neither meets the criteria of a rogue state in the way that, say, Iraq does. Both have democratically elected governments. But within both countries, domestic pressure as well as strategic interests overrode the anticipated damage of internationally imposed sanctions in their decisions to detonate fissionable material.

The final category, and the subject of this essay, is the *terrorist* rogue state. This deadly manifestation in the emerging world order has captured Washington's attention. These nation-states fail to comply with the rules of international law. Their behavior is defiant and belligerent. They promote radical ideologies. They share an anti-Western bias, in general, and an anti-American hatred, in particular. Rogue political systems vary, but their leaders share a common antipathy toward their citizens' participating in the political process. They suppress human and civil rights as do diplomatic rogue states, but their international bellicosity is the key variable drawing our attention to them.

Rogue nations often possess larger conventional military forces than their national defense warrants, sponsor international terrorism, and strive to obtain weapons of mass destruction. Violent acts toward nearby states are attributable to rogues such as Iran, Iraq, Libya, Syria, Cuba, Sudan, and North Korea, which are classified by the U.S. Department of State as terrorist states. Although Iraq, Iran, and North Korea have captured the lion's share of Washington's antiterrorist attention during the 1990s, the other states have supplied "passive" forms of support to terrorism in the form of training facilities and safe havens for subversive agents. Afghanistan's willingness to lend sanctuary to Osama bin Laden, the exiled Saudi Arabian businessman turned terrorist, makes it a terrorist-supporting state capable of inflicting harm on the United States and its citizens. The peril posed by rogues to Americans and U.S. interests has intensified with the dispersal of weapons of mass destruction following the dissolution of the Soviet Union.

Other threats have arisen from terrorist individuals or movements made up of Islamic fundamentalists or other ideologically charged cults such as Aum Shinrikyo, whose manufacture and lethal use of sarin nerve gas shocked Japanese society, or the militia movement within the United States. Attacks on the World Trade Center in New York City and the Oklahoma federal building only confirmed suspicions of our vulnerability. Increasing the uneasiness felt in our country and other societies was that bomb-making information appeared on the Internet, open to anyone with a computer. When rogue governments aid paramilitary parties in the pursuit of terrorism, then the threat moves from the nonstate perpetrator to the government-sponsored category.

The increased emphasis given to global economic issues after the end of the cold war gave birth to the fashionable notion that economic preeminence is more important than politico-military considerations in international politics. That nostrum ignores the fundamental fact that global markets depend on a secure international system. It is geopolitical power, of which economic well-being is one factor, that undergirds the global system. Rogue adversaries threaten the global equilibrium on which the United States and other nations base their commerce, access to resources and financial capital, human interchange, and security.

Rogue assaults on accepted international conduct disrupts peace and stability. Mussolini's invasion of Ethiopia in 1935 went a long way toward unraveling European peace, in large part because the League of Nations failed to rally effective opposition. Saddam Hussein's military incursion into Kuwait likewise tossed the Persian Gulf states into turmoil and shattered the dawn of the post-Soviet order. But unlike Italy's prewar aggression, Iraq's was met, defeated, and turned back by an American-led coalition. This was the proper reaction to Baghdad's attack. Lawlessness feeds on itself if allowed to spread unchecked.

America's Role in a Rogue World

As the remaining superpower, the United States faces a unique political environment. It is both the world's reigning hegemon and sometime villain. America's economic, military, and technological prowess endows it with what Secretary of State Madeleine K. Albright has termed *indispensability*. Whatever the political upheaval or humanitarian crisis, other states expect the United States to solve the world's problems and to dispense good deeds. Those expectations arise from the fact that America has often come to the rescue in the past and that the United States is not a traditional nation. America is the embodiment of the idea that a free people share sovereignty, with rights and obligations, as set forth in a written constitution that has strengthened over the past two hundred years. Unlike most traditional nations, we do not share a common ancestry. Thus America seeks to advance ideals. Our national goals encompass more than geopolitical ends, which is why Americans are unsettled by the slaughter of innocents in faraway lands. American foreign policy debates and interventionist decisions usually include democratic values as well as our vital overseas interests.

Overseas engagement, whether military, diplomatic or economic, has indeed steadily become an integral part of America's external policy during this century. Washington's leadership and power proved decisive from World War I to the Persian Gulf war. In each of these major conflicts, the United States fought as member of an international coalition and its role has been pivotal. Despite domestic isolationist pulls, the United States, more than ever, is *the* key international player. No other state or global body commands similar world standing. The United Nations, on which so much optimistic expectation rested following World War II, is judged ineffectual in major crises. Even after the conclusion of bipolarism, the United Nations Security Council suffers from nationalistic divisions. The anticipation of a veto from one of the other four permanent members (Britain, China, France, Russia) holds American initiatives hostage to a watered-down consensus. (Likewise, America's veto power works to constrain the ambitions of China and Russia in the Security Council.)

Hard realities, not mere altruism, mean that America must act not like a policeman but like a sheriff in the old Western frontier towns, acting alone on occasion, relying on deputies or long-standing allies, or looking for a posse among regional partners. Or, in some cases, it may look for another sheriff, or regional power, to organize local forces.[3] It cannot allow desperadoes to run loose without encouraging other outlaws to test the limits of law and order. History instructs us that the U.S. withdrawal from world problems, leaving Europeans and Asians to their own devices in the 1930s, led to the rise of militarism and aggression. Aloofness from international politics is simply not a viable option.

We benefit materially from a stable and peaceful world. Our economic and political health depend on cross-border trade and international stability. The percentage of our gross domestic product (GDP) based on foreign trade has doubled since 1970. In 1997, exports alone reached 12 percent of GDP and imports totaled 13 percent. Although exports and imports combined accounted for one-quarter of GDP, total trade accounted for more than one-third of the average U.S. national income per capita ($19,700). The United States, which accounts for about 14 percent of total world trade (exports and imports), is the world's largest exporter of goods and services, $933 billion in 1997. It is not in our interest to stand aside while rogue behavior unravels a region's trade, economic, and human networks.

In today's globally interconnected world, events on one side of the planet can influence actions on the other side, meaning that how the United States responds to a regional rogue has worldwide implications. Rogue leaders draw conclusions from weak responses to aggression. That Iraq's president, Saddam Hussein, escaped unpunished for his invasion of Kuwait no doubt emboldened the Yugoslav president, Slobodan Milosevic, in his campaign to extirpate Muslims from Bosnia-Herzegovina in pursuit of a greater Serbia. Deterring security threats is a valuable mechanism to maintain peace, as witnessed by the cold war, and it may afford the only realistic option available. But in dealing with rogue states deterrence and containment may not be enough. Before NATO intervened in the Bosnia imbroglio in 1995, to take one example, the ethno-nationalist conflict raised the specter of a wider war, drawing in the neighboring countries of Greece, Turkey, and Russia.

Political inaction creates vacuums, which can suck in states to fill the void. Although the United States does not want to be the world's sheriff, living in a world without law and order is not an auspicious prospect. This said, it must be emphasized that the United States ought not intervene militarily in every conflict or humanitarian crisis. Indeed, it should pick its interventions with great care. Offering Washington's good offices to mediate disputes in distant corners is one thing; dispatching armed forces to far-flung deserts, jungles, or mountains is quite another.

A global doctrine setting forth all-inclusive guidelines is difficult to cast in stone. Containment, the doctrine articulated in response to Soviet global ambitions, offered a realistic guideline for policymakers. A similar response to rogue states cannot be easily cloned for each contingency but may require the United States to corral allies or partners into a unified policy, as circumstances dictate. But watching rogue behavior with complacency or relying on the United Nations courts disaster in the age of weapons of mass destruction.

Most incidents of civil turmoil need not engage U.S. military forces. Regrettable as the bloody civil war in Sri Lanka is, it demands no American intervention, for the ethnic conflict between the secessionist Tamil minority and the Sinhalese majority is largely an internal affair. Political turmoil in Cambodia is largely a domestic problem. Even the civil war in the Congo, which has drawn in small military forces from Uganda, Rwanda, Angola, and Zimbabwe, is a Central African affair. Aside from international prodding, the simmering Congolese fighting is better left to Africans to resolve than to outsiders. In the case of the decades-long slaughter in southern Sudan, the United States can serve a humanitarian cause by calling international attention to Khartoum's genocide of Christian and animist peoples. These types of conflicts, however, do not endanger U.S. strategic interests, undermine regional order, threaten global commercial relationships, or, realistically, call for direct humanitarian intervention. No weapons of mass destruction menace surrounding peoples or allies. Thus, there is no compelling reason for U.S. military deployment.

Terrorist rogue states, in contrast, must be confronted with robust measures, or the world will go down the same path as it did in the 1930s, when Europe and the United States allowed Nazi Germany to propagate its ideology across half a dozen states, to rearm for a war of conquest, and to intimidate the democracies into appeasement. Rogue states push the world toward anarchy and away from stability. Zbigniew Brzezinski, the former national security adviser to President Carter, cited preventing global anarchy as one of the two goals of "America's global engagement, namely, that of forging an enduring framework of global geopolitical cooperation." The other key goal is "impeding the emergence of a power rival."[4]

Former Secretary of State George Shultz has cogently linked force and diplomacy in practice and in word. He persuasively argued the principle while in office and later in his memoir that force should be used not as a last resort but as an integral component of diplomacy. In defending the 1983 combat assault on the island of Grenada to rescue American hostages and halt the spread of communism in the Caribbean, for example, he wrote in *Turmoil and Triumph*, his personal account of his years in the Reagan administration:

> The use of force, and the credible threat of the use of force, are legitimate instruments of national policy and should be viewed as such. . . . The use of force obviously should not be taken lightly, but better to use force when you *should* rather than when you *must; last* means *no other*, and by that time the level of force and the risk involved may have multiplied many times over.[5]

The Clinton administration, in contrast, severed the nexus between power and diplomacy in dealing with rogue states, with a resulting decline in U.S. credibility. Its mishandling of crises in Iraq, North Korea, and the Balkans furnishes ample negative lessons for diplomatic relations with rogue governments. Rather than build public support for a respected overseas policy, the poll-driven Clinton White House pursued the lines of least resistance. It avoided shaping international policy among a disinterested electorate, devoted episodic attention to rogue transgressions, and repeatedly vacillated on the use of military force to achieve its diplomatic ends. Rogues played off American predilections for their own goals, leaving Washington appearing incoherent, hesitant, and ineffectual.

Law, Diplomacy, and Power

Three central concepts undergird the available instruments that serve U.S. foreign policymakers confronting a renegade regime: law, diplomacy, and power. Law stands at one end of the policy spectrum and power at the other, with diplomacy in the middle, thus representing a "response ramp" from the least severe to the most severe tool. Legal remedies constitute the cheapest and least aggressive reaction; power, in its various forms, is the most drastic weapon in a nation's arsenal. Diplomatic means encompass a wide range of options, from recalling ambassadors to closing embassies. Moving steadily from one end of the spectrum to the other is ineffective against rogues, however, failing to capture the complexity of dealing effectively with outlaws.

To deal with outlaws, the tools should be applied as nearly simultaneously as feasible. Thus, at the same time that the United States imposes sanctions, it should, for instance, establish a credible force and bolster internal movements opposed to the despotic leader. We *must* implement these options together because they each, of necessity, depend on the other in extreme cases. Careful diplomacy is required to fashion a consensus on international law and build support for strong action. Law is enforceable only within a structure that delivers consequences. Likewise, accepted international codes serve to justify resorting to force or other hostile diplomatic instruments. Thus, law, diplomacy, and power are logically interconnected to, and reinforce the effects of, one another. Unfortunately, rogue regimes reject the underlying concepts of normal international laws and established diplomacy. They assert their own sovereignty even when punitive political or military intervention is justified. But the right of self-protection assures the United States of legitimacy. It is acknowledged that international law is a key factor in foreign policy. Diplomacy is most effective when it accords with the norms of international law. Although the United States must be prepared to act alone in confronting rogue states, it is important to avoid acting outside established international standards, lest it be considered no better than the terrorist regimes it wishes to condemn.

Instruments of Power and Diplomacy

When a rogue player provokes an international crisis, the response is often that something needs to be done. Several forceful foreign policy strategies represent measures short of declared war. Each will be explored and evaluated in the balance of this essay. They can be summarized as follows:

- Sanctions and isolation to achieve containment and economic damage
- International courts and domestic prosecution
- Shows of strength and armed interventions
- Support for opposition movements or covert operations

These stiff measures can be complemented by inducements to mend a rogue state's behavior. Thus carrots can be offered in a carefully crafted approach along with sticks. But the danger in offering blandishments to a rogue state is that it may misread the signals as appeasement. For example, before its invasion of Kuwait, Iraq misinterpreted as weakness the Bush administration's private expressions to Baghdad of continued friendship and wrongly concluded that Washington's public opposition to its planned invasion was mere window dressing for the international community.

The many nonstringent instruments of U.S. diplomacy are ineffective in aggravated disputes with rogue states. The U. S. Department of State's Advisory Committee on International Economic Policy released a report entitled "U.S Foreign Policy Tools: An Illustrative Matrix of Selected Options" in 1997. It listed numerous responses, positive and negative, that the United States can initiate to influence another state's behavior. The positive incentives run from accrediting ambassadors and sending warm proclamations from the executive branch to shipping military equipment with congressional approval or exchanging presidential visits between the United States and a foreign country. Other positive inducements include rescheduling loans, trade opportunities, and aid concessions.

These displays of warm relations and positive actions can be countermatched with disapproving symbols and firm reactions for a state's bad conduct. Again, the range stretches from mild disapproval, such as the reduction of U.S. embassy staff in a foreign capital, to escalating warlike actions leading ultimately to total war. Since making war against even a rogue state is an extreme step, it is necessary to contemplate ways to attain our diplomatic goals with measures short of war.

SANCTIONS

Economic sanctions, as a form of pressure against another state, have been employed as instruments of foreign policy since classical antiquity. Ancient Athens, to illustrate, retaliated against Megara for its assistance to Corinth at the battle of Sybota by excluding Megarians from Athenian ports and markets. In early periods, sanctions usually accompanied military conflicts. But after World War I, economic sanctions as a standalone policy gradually became substitutes for military action. Since the costs of war are high and diplomatic protests are weak, sanctions became a middle instrument between the two. Economic sanctions entail a government-instigated withdrawal, or the threat of withdrawal, of customary financial or trade patterns with the targeted country. They exact not only economic costs but also political ones. Sanctions are a part of a containment strategy. By implication, sanctions stigmatize a target state and restrict its international relations.

Military sanctions fall into a somewhat different category than economic ones in that they seek to deprive an adversary of the war matériel or arms technology with direct military application. (Since some advanced technology has dual-use capabilities, civilian as well as military, these items are often lumped within the economic category by states introducing sanctions.) A strong and popular case can usually be made for military sanctions. American citizens, if not always U.S. arms exporters, accept the necessity of limiting the transfer of military hardware or advanced technology to a real or potential enemy. Realistically, militarily applicable equipment has been difficult to deny a rogue indefinitely, if only because competitor states such as China and Russia have often sold it to prohibited buyers such as Iran and Iraq.

Out of a broad array of options, economic sanctions have become a weapon of choice of the United States and the international community. This development raised opposition from domestic businesses, which favor sanctions for *trade* purposes but not for *foreign policy* reasons. Antisanction business lobbyists thus mounted a public relations campaign aginst the imposition of U.S. unilateral embargoes for foreign policy ends. Based on a study by the National Association of Manufacturers, USA Engage, a coalition of American businesses, contends that Washington resorted to sanctions sixty-one times between 1993 and 1996. But a senatorial rebuttal argued persuasively that Congress and the executive branch unilaterally imposed sanctions in only nine new instances. The balance came from U.S. compliance with U.N. sanctions, restrictions on American foreign aid, and bans on military sales or a specific foreign company or person.[6]

States or international organizations apply economic sanctions against a targeted government for many different goals. Among the most prevalent are to further military actions, destabilize a government, deter objectionable behavior, halt proliferation of weapons of mass destruction, settle expropriation disputes, combat terrorism, safeguard the environment, protect human rights, and demonstrate resolve. One important study of sanctions concluded that economic embargoes have been most frequently instituted by the United States to help destabilize foreign governments. This study's authors hold that Washington has resorted to destabilization efforts on fifteen separate occasions, playing at least a modest role in toppling Rafael Trujillo, the Dominican Republic's strongman, in 1961; in overthrowing Salvador Allende, the Chilean president, in 1973; and in the 1990 election loss by the Sandanistas in Nicaragua.[7] A more recent example of sanctions used for political destabilization is Iraq, where the jury is still out on the result of economic warfare, if any, on the projected end of Saddam Hussein's rule.

In the following discussion, various objections will be enumerated to an overreliance on sanctions as a foreign policy tool. Despite their failings, however, it is clear that sanctions can be used effectively and must remain part of our diplomatic arsenal.

Selected Case Studies

Sanctions alone are not a fail-safe mechanism for getting rid of unsavory rulers. The record of sanctions, in fact, is quite mixed. U.S. economic restrictions have failed to dislodge or bend communist dictators such as Fidel Castro in Cuba and Kim Il Sung (or his son Kim Jong Il) in North Korea after decades of imposition. Slobodan Milosevic in the Federal Republic of Yugoslavia, a more recent target of sanctions, has survived military setbacks, along with economic quarantine and inflation, which have decimated the wealth of the country's middle class. Only a U.S. military invasion of Panama achieved Washington's goal of ousting General Manuel Noriega, who withstood years of U.S. economic pressure. Sanction-induced governmental shipwrecks are long shots against most entrenched strongmen.

Economic coercion cannot administer a fatal bite in the flanks of determined regimes because the teeth are not up to the task. A state under economic siege can endure economic dislocation because other countries may not cooperate in an economic and trade lockout; "black knights" pursue their own economic and political agendas. For example, European states continue to trade with Cuba, despite strict U.S. economic sanctions against the Castro regime.

Sanctions can also motivate strong nationalistic responses in an embattled country. Citizens rally to support their government and seek ways to circumvent commercial problems. Italians, for example, redoubled their support of Mussolini when the League of Nations instituted sanctions in the mid-1930s for Italy's invasion of Ethiopia. Similar reactions took place over U.S. sanctions against Nicaragua in the 1980s, the United Nations' economic quarantine of Rhodesia (1965–79), and Soviet embargoes (1948–55) on Yugoslavia, following its break with Moscow. Sanctions against even unpopular leaders, such as Fidel Castro and Saddam Hussein generate anti-American sentiments and provide a plausible rationale for why Cuba's economy is performing poorly. Citizens are persuaded to blame outsiders for shortages instead of shortcomings in a command-and-control economy. North Korea, arguably the most repressive society on the planet, blames the United States and its other adversaries for its economic and agricultural problems rather than its own rigid autarkic practices.

Economic sanctions against rogue regimes also result in limited payoffs because dictators are usually indifferent to the sufferings of their own people. One striking case of hard-heartedness is Saddam Hussein, who builds palaces and armaments while ordinary Iraqis want for food and medicine. North Korea's Kim Jong Il and Libya's Muammar Qaddafi, like numerous other despots, manifest no feeling for their countrymen's suffering because of government policies, sanctions or not.

Unintended consequences often flow from sanctions; instead of

Using Power and Diplomacy to Deal with Rogue States 17

political shipwreck, they have motivated people to improvise and develop economic self-sufficiency. One classic illustration of this process is the former Rhodesia (now Zimbabwe). When first Britain and then the United Nations placed sanctions on the breakaway Rhodesian government, the landlocked African state found itself almost friendless in the world community. During the decade from 1965 to 1975, Rhodesia transformed its economy from a near-total dependence on imported manufactured goods in exchange for raw materials to a high degree of self-sufficiency. Only oil production and industrial machinery eluded Rhodesian enterprise. Moreover, Rhodesia's economy initially increased its productivity.

Rhodesia was also aided by the sanction-busting South Africa and Portuguese-ruled Mozambique, which served as conduits for importing petroleum products and other vital products and harbors for exporting Rhodesian goods. For more than a decade, the European-ruled state held out. In the end, the African majority came to power because the white minority government experienced a host of other challenges, including a widespread guerrilla war in much of the countryside. By the early 1970s the drastic hike in oil prices had further taxed Rhodesian resources. African rule came to Mozambique in 1975, thereby closing off a key trade artery. Finally, South Africa abandoned Rhodesia in a calculated bid to win world approval despite its own internationally censured racial policies toward its African majority. The economic siege of Rhodesia contributed to its defeat, but it's doubtful if sanctions alone would have determined the outcome. It took a rural insurgency coupled with adverse international circumstances.[8]

Even without clear-cut victories, sanctions still can be an effective, if limited, weapon in the United States' diplomatic arsenal. Sanctions, if properly enforced, raise havoc with an embattled economy. Although they are powerless to turn back fierce aggression like Iraq's invasion of Kuwait, they can raise difficulties for contentious states. Securing the suspension of sanctions on natural gas and heating oil to Serbia during the bitter winter of 1995 made Milosevic more amenable to compromise at Dayton.[9] Economic sanctions and political containment squeezed Libya to the point that it openly discussed having two of its citizens stand trial in The Hague for bombing Pan Am flight 103 over Scotland in 1988. Libyan strongman Qaddafi floated the idea of making a deal with the United States in return for dropping sanctions in mid-1998.

Even less than watertight restrictions interfere with normal business mechanisms, adding extra costs and economic inefficiencies to the sanctioned country. That economic coercion can be effective is borne out by the evidence that resentful embargoed countries struggle to have sanctions lifted, reviling America for imposing them. They pay fortunes to Washington lobbyists to work the political process to terminate economic pressure. Yet these targeted regimes at the same time insist that sanctions fail to alter their policies. They complain that U.S. embargoes succeed only in starving children and hurting the poor. But economic sanctions do damage economies and do morally stigmatize their targets, making them popular instruments in Washington.

Opponents and Guidelines

Economic sanctions, however, can generate determined U.S. domestic opposition. A recent case in point is the home-front reaction to Washington's prescription for nuclear tests on the Indian subcontinent. In the wake of first India and then Pakistan exploding atomic devices in May 1998, the United States put in place sanctions against the two countries under the 1994 Arms Export Control Act, which punishes governments for detonating thermonuclear mechanisms. This legislation suspended trade credits, private bank loans, loan guarantees, and support loans from international financial institutions.

Little time was lost in backing away from these draconian approaches, however, in response to opposition from the farm belt, which had already suffered declining sales of agricultural products to the economically faltering Asia. The Clinton administration thus endorsed a resumption of World Bank lending to India, citing an exemption in the export law for humanitarian assistance. Next, two months after the tests, the U.S. Senate voted ninety-eight to zero to exempt grain exports from the sanctions against New Delhi and Islamabad. Soon afterward the House of Representatives voted to curtail the sanctions by a similarly lopsided margin. Presidential and congressional action thus lifted the most severe economic penalties, leaving in place the little-used restrictions on arms sales. (India buys few American weapons, and Pakistan had already incurred a cutoff in U.S military imports in 1990 for its suspected development of nuclear devices.)

Looking to the November 1998 congressional elections, officeholders moved quickly to remove potentially damaging sanctions from voters' minds. After the midterm congressional elections, Clinton waived some sanctions under authority granted from Capitol Hill, ostensibly because India and Pakistan promised to stop nuclear testing but not to stop production of fissile material or to forgo deployment of atomic weapons. Farmers in U.S. wheat-growing states, feeling the economic pinch, lobbied successfully for an end to grain sanctions. In this case sanctions were viewed as hurting specific groups or businesses within the sender state as much as the targets. But most sanctions have not been gutted by domestic pressure. In some cases, as with the powerful Cuban lobby in southern Florida, sanctions have been kept in place for domestic political reasons.

The recent overreliance on sanctions by Washington and their imperfect outcomes have generated determined congressional and business opposition, which has correctly pressured for a review of sanction policy and its near-indiscriminate reliance on economic embargoes. Economic bans have been overused, often appeasing domestic critics rather than attaining a political objective. Economic sanctions have additional failings, including their indefinite duration. Once applied, sanctions often stay in force beyond the expectations of success or recognized purpose.

Engaging some closed societies in commerce, cultural, and human exchanges will do more to open and expose their repressive regimes to the winds of change than walling them up behind sanctions and containment measures. Soviet Russia fell apart in some measure because of the exposure of its citizens to Western society. The same fate awaits two other relics of East-West competition—Cuba and North Korea. Neither sanctions nor containment have brought down these Stalinesque anomalies. Ending sanctions against Havana and Pyongyang should be seen not as American weakness but as the application of another weapon—engagement leading to reintegration into the competitive global economy. Our allies would welcome this activist approach over the passive method of sanctions, particularly European states whose corporations already do business with Cuba and resent American financial claims on them for utilizing expropriated American property. South Korea's new president, Kim Dae Jung, liberalized restrictive policies on investments and family contacts with the North in the first months of his administration in early 1998.

Because policymakers must choose between war or words, they often resort to the low-cost sanctions option. Like most diplomatic tools, sanctions are sometimes effective and sometimes not. Overuse certainly dulls their efficacy. Economic pressure is most effective when combined with other policies. Sanctions should be used sparingly and only when other diplomatic options seem unlikely to succeed. Washington should seek international participation before promulgating unilateral sanctions. But achieving collective action may prove impossible, as it has in most cases, and its absence should not deter the United States when the stakes are high.

Unless we are willing to act unilaterally, our response to security threats or humanitarian outrages will be subject to another state's veto, and we will end up striving for consensus rather than our own strategic goals. Sanctions should be designed to spare the innocent people of a target state unnecessary hardship and to inflict pain on the regime by restricting technology transfers rather than food and medicine. Sanctions should exact maximum leverage on the target while minimizing the cost to American citizens and U.S. allies. The executive and legislative branches should subject sanctions to periodic review to determine their effectiveness. Ineffective sanctions should be dropped or refocused.

The gravest shortcoming of sanctions lies in the political cover they afford politicians for not adopting a more meaningful course of action. Economic embargoes fulfill the need to respond to a challenge, but they alone can rarely achieve an ambitious objective. Against rogue regimes, they are only a first response, not an endgame. Sanctions must not be an easy substitute for a well-conceived strategy.

International Courts and Domestic Prosecution of War Crimes

The postbipolar political landscape affords a fresh opportunity to use U.S. and international laws to combat rogue leaders. Previously, the American and Soviet spheres of influence shielded such figures because of their usefulness to one side or the other. Now despotic leaders or individual terrorists who break global statutes outlawing war crimes and genocide face the prospect of arrest, trial, and punishment at the hands of international tribunals or even U.S. courts. In 1984 and 1986, Congress enacted laws making it a crime to harm an American citizen or attack an American business for political aims anywhere in the world. Congress also authorized the FBI to investigate those crimes, arrest the perpetrators, and transport them for trial in U.S. courts. It also established a rewards program, whereby the government could offer up to $2 million for the prevention of or information about political violence leading to the arrest of those responsible for incidents against Americans or their property overseas. Washington recently increased the price on Osama bin Ladin to $5 million to demonstrate its determination and to sweeten the offer for would-be collaborators. It also extended the rewards program to the capture of indicted war criminals, even when Americans were not the victims.

These laws afford Washington effective tools against state or nonstate actors. For example, the United States has apprehended, tried, and convicted in a federal court Ramzi Yousef, a native of Pakistan who masterminded the 1993 World Trade Center truck bombing. With help from foreign contacts, FBI agents also captured, put on trial, and convicted Mir Amal Kansi of assassinating two CIA employees outside their Virginia headquarters in 1993.

The precedents for bringing war criminals to justice began after World War II, when an agreement was reached among the United States, the Soviet Union, Britain, and France to establish an international military tribunal. The agreement set forth the jurisdiction and functions of the tribunal as well as the crimes for which the defendants might be held individually responsible. The ensuing Nuremberg trials convicted and punished almost a score of Nazi military and civilian leaders for crimes against peace, war crimes, and crimes against humanity. A similar postwar trial took place in Tokyo for Japanese war criminals.

Simultaneous with the war crimes trials, the U.N. General Assembly unanimously resolved that genocide was "a crime under international law" for which private individuals as well as public officials were punishable. Two years later, in 1948, the General Assembly adopted the Convention on the Prevention and Punishment of the Crime of Genocide, which defined genocide as killing or harming of a group of people so as to entail its destruction. The convention entrusts punishment primarily to the courts of the concerned country, but if they fail to act, then the incidents can be reported to the International Court of Justice for possible action.

After the Soviet Union's breakup, the times seemed propitious to refocus attention on violations of international norms, for the Soviets' removal from international politics coincided with the unfolding of serious breaches in civilized conduct. In the early 1990s, large-scale killings, war-related rapes, and "ethnic cleansing," first in southeastern Europe and then in Central Africa, riveted world attention on the necessity to bring the perpetrators to justice. The United Nations Security Council set up the International Criminal Tribunal in 1993 at

The Hague to try war crimes cases arising from the conflict in the former Yugoslavia. By fall of 1998, thirty-five of seventy-nine publicly indicted war criminals had been brought to justice at The Hague for the 1991–95 war. Three—two Bosnian Muslims and one Croat—as of this writing, had been convicted and sentenced for torture and killings. But the majority of the indicted suspects are Bosnian Serbs, while most of the tens of thousands of victims came from the Muslim and Croat communities. The trials are proceeding.

The Security Council also established an international tribunal to investigate mass killings in Rwanda in 1994. Four years later, it sentenced the former prime minister of Rwanda, Jean Kambanda, to life in prison for his part in the mass murder of a reported half million Tutsi by their fellow Hutu countrymen. He was the first to be convicted of the crime of genocide, as defined in the postwar genocide convention. The three-judge panel, which was based in Arusha, Tanzania, also convicted Jean-Paul Akayesu, a former small-town mayor, for the crime of genocide and for the first time included rape as a genocide crime. The Rwandan verdicts and The Hague trials demonstrate an effective means of dealing with war crimes when national courts lack the capacity or inclination.

Faintheartedness in apprehending those accused of genocide ruptures the international judicial system and discredits the political framework of civilized states, as well as undercutting American efforts to defeat rogue conduct. One egregious illustration of this lapse is the failure to apprehend two of the foremost Serbian war criminals. In July 1995, an international criminal tribunal indicted Radovan Karadzic, the wartime political leader of the Bosnian Serbs, and General Ratko Mladic, the Serbs' military head, on charges of genocide, crimes against humanity, and war crimes. The Dayton Accords, signed in December 1995 to bring peace to the former Yugoslavia, contained provisions for apprehending Dr. Karadzic and General Mladic, along with some seventy other indicted war criminals. The Hague also contended that the United Nations had a legal obligation to arrest both men, and many

U.S. officials felt that they also had a moral obligation to bring them to justice.

After numerous opportunities and several millions of dollars spent in training for missions to place the two major figures in custody, Karadzic and Mladic remain at large. On more than one occasion, NATO troops could have arrested them, and the United States made elaborate plans for military operations to capture them but abandoned the preparations in mid-1998 as too risky. What the United States and NATO feared were reprisals by angry Serbs as well as an unraveling of the peace agreement or a bloodbath if the operation went awry. The Clinton administration hinted that it will await the slow erosion of Karadzic and Mladic's support, as funds and adherents dwindle.

The power base of both men, Clinton officials hoped, will be subject to laws of diminishing popularity and receding finances with the passage of time out of office and the rise of other political figures. Prospects for a gradual Serbian disenchantment with their wartime leaders appear faint at this writing. Be that as it may, the Clinton administration abdicated a moral and legal obligation. Had it led a NATO operation to bring Karadzic and Mladic to justice, a powerful message would have been sent to current and future perpetrators of mass murder. Such a message might lessen or even prevent human rights abuses. Leaving indicted mass killers to wither on the vine signals that justice is being denied.

The International Criminal Court

The U.N. Security Council, where the United States enjoys a veto as one of the five permanent members, set up both the Bosnia and the Rwanda tribunals, thus allowing the United States to guide and protect its global role as the sole superpower. Efforts toward founding a supranational court, however, are seen as endangering U.S. sovereignty and security.

Proponents of such a supranational court, to be called the International Criminal Court (ICC), met in Rome during June and July 1998. Delegates from more than 150 countries finalized language and adopted a treaty establishing the ICC as an independent and permanent international court for prosecuting war criminals, genocide, and crimes against humanity. Unlike the separation of duties under the American legal system, the ICC empowers judges and agents to investigate, prosecute, hand down judgments, determine sentences, and even hear appeals to its own pronouncements. Its jurisdiction could extend to U.S. territory and thereby threaten American sovereignty.

Unlike the ad hoc tribunal set up by the Security Council for specific crimes, the United States enjoys no protection from the interference of an international bureaucracy, unaccountable to any electorate. The possibility of a U.S. veto, such as the one it wields in the Security Council, has been structurally denied, as were procedures that have protected the United States from the whims of the U.N. General Assembly. Washington's military operations, often conducted for larger international goals, would be subject to ICC prosecution for aggression or interference in another country. At best, Washington might feel constrained in implementing military actions; at worst, American civilian officials and military officers, after executing armed operations, might have to stand trial before judges drawn from all states, including some of the most repressive, undemocratic societies on earth.

The Clinton administration, which had sponsored efforts and encouraged prospects for a supranational criminal court for five years, felt compelled to abstain from joining the ICC. American delegates concluded, too late, that articles establishing the international court violated the U.S. Constitution, undermined effective American actions around the world, and stood no chance of passage in the U.S. Senate. Although the United States abandoned the ICC treaty, it faces a plethora of future problems for its part in assembling a Frankenstein monster all too likely to turn on its creator.

The United States must do everything in its power to constrict the growth of the ICC, which will come into force once sixty nations ratify the statute. It must isolate it, deny its legitimacy, reject its jurisdiction, refute its decisions, and reduce its status. In the past, skittishness about international courts has led the United States to refuse to recognize decisions handed down by the International Court of Justice (ICJ). Commonly known as the World Court, the ICJ was established to adjudicate disputes among nations, not to try individuals. It has handed down decisions outlawing the use of nuclear weapons and condemning as unlawful the U.S. sanctions on Nicaragua during Washington's conflict with the Sandinista government during the 1980s, prompting the United States to withdraw from mandatory jurisdiction.[10] The United States will have to adopt a similar policy of not recognizing judgments by the ICC.

Washington must counterbalance its attack on the ICC by supporting the current system of tribunals crafted by the U.N. Security Council. Such tribunals, like those trying cases from Rwanda or Bosnia, are charged with defined authority, which prevents them from going beyond their original mandate. Their flaws, including charges of lacking impartiality and needing greater financial assistance, can be corrected. They can be more frequently impaneled so as to confront the charge that there are too few to handle the many cases of war crimes and crimes against humanity.

The international outcry against war crimes and their perpetrators gives U.S. diplomacy a club to wield against rogue rulers who commit genocide against their own citizens or other national, religious, and ethnic communities. By using them properly, Washington can add U.S. courts and case-specific international tribunals to its antirogue arsenal. Saddam Hussein's well-documented atrocities make him a prime candidate for an international indictment. Like economic sanctions, which are also nonmilitary steps, law is a powerful instrument that can help constrain, stigmatize, and isolate a rogue target. An indicted leader, even if unable to be brought to justice, becomes an international outlaw. And unlike sanctions, indicted war criminals face genuine threats to their own personal safety and freedom.

Assassinations and Asset Seizures

Murderous rogues and individual terrorist acts have again raised the question of using political assassination as a tool to deal with the menace of terrorism. Ever since President Ford's 1976 Executive Order No. 12333 prohibiting the government from abetting in the assassination of political or terrorist leaders, there have been calls to repeal it. Both Presidents Reagan and Clinton, however, reissued the executive order banning murder, yet both administrations have ordered deadly counteractions against the headquarters of terrorist figures. Reagan struck at Qaddafi, and Clinton fired cruise missiles at bin Laden. Despite such concrete steps against terrorism, however, critics still seek to revoke our self-declared restraint on political murder. But although there are some instances where the prohibition could be judged a hindrance to eliminating terrorists, in less hypothetical cases, it presents little practical problem. After all, nation-states retain the lawful right to self-defense under international conventions.

Realistically, a presidential order to hit back militarily at a rogue command center or to engineer a coup may well result in the death of a despot as a part of the operation. In these scenarios, the mission does not directly target a rogue for execution. Rather, it is a legitimate act of self-protection to strike preemptively at a security threat, such as the U.S. cruise missile assault on the pharmaceutical plant in Sudan. If a rogue leader is killed as a by-product of a larger operation, such as missile assault or commando raid to disrupt an assassin's camp, this does not breach the self-imposed executive stipulation as, say, a calculated sniper ambush to assassinate a rogue figure might. His removal would simply be the fortunes of politics or the uncontrollable outcome of a violent clash. Thus, it appears unlikely that U.S. operations have been, or are likely to be, hampered by a broadly interpreted presidential fiat.

A more fundamental issue, which is obscured by the debate on the assassination executive order, revolves around the dilemma of whether it is more effective to adhere to legal practices or instigate extralegal operations to fight terrorism. It is tempting to act outside the law when grappling with murderous rogue conduct, for some consider the legal process to be cumbersome and ill-designed for the exigencies of combating political violence. In this view, the normal legal safeguards, due process, and rules of evidence in courtroom procedure hinder rather than assist in the struggle against roguery. But if a U.S. administration behaves as a terrorist, then it forfeits its legitimacy as a government. Sir Robert Thompson, who wrote about the necessity of the government's adherence to the law and legal procedures in defeating communist violence in Malaya and the Philippines during the 1950s, believed that legal methods played a major role in discrediting the communist guerrillas, making them appear as criminals rather than patriots in the public's mind.[11]

Bringing rogues to trial in civil courts, *whenever possible*, trying them as criminals, and convicting and sentencing them as lawbreakers gains sympathy and support, even from those not directly involved in the conflict. Adhering to established legal procedures enhances the legitimacy of the American cause and criminalizes deplorable behavior, denying martyrdom to all but the most committed followers. None of this argument should be construed to mean that the United States should not unleash severe military actions to destroy state and nonstate terrorist centers. It must strike against perpetrators of political violence for the purposes of deterrence, prevention, and punishment. But when circumstances permit the taking into custody of rogue players or terrorists, it is good policy to bring them to justice rather than conducting a summary execution.

This method of law enforcement achieves a powerful psychological victory, wherein the government is seen as the protector of societal principles and the terrorist is cast as antisocial and a violator of international norms and civilized conduct, deserving legally sanctioned punishment. Had President Manuel Noriega been executed during the course of the Panama invasion, he might now be seen by ordinary

Panamanians as a martyred freedom fighter instead of a narcotics trafficker in a Miami prison.

Another legal remedy in the fight against rogues is seizing the financial assets they use to perpetrate their lethal activities, such as the U.S. pursuit of bin Ladin's banking deposits and business profits. Although tracking a terrorist's financial resources and banking networks is a difficult process, U.S. spy agencies can use computers to tap into foreign bank accounts to trace the flow of funds or even make them disappear. Naturally, there is a reluctance to report on the progress of these measures.[12] In the past, the United States froze Iranian assets in American banks following the takeover of the U.S. embassy in Tehran in 1979 and Iraqi foreign accounts in the wake of its Kuwait invasion. These stiff approaches add to the countermeasures against a state's deadly overseas enterprises.

Nonmilitary options such as criminal trials and asset seizures are necessary and useful instruments against rogues but not normally sufficient to eject them from office. More direct applications of power must be harnessed to antirogue statecraft.

Shows of Strength and Armed Interventions to Coerce or Eliminate Rogue Governments

Rogue regimes, by their very nature, are less persuaded by appeals to the fine points of international law and customary diplomatic practices than by armed force. Coercive diplomacy is initiated after, or in response to, a hostile action, whereas deterring a foe dissuades him from undertaking an activity by threatening retaliation. But the principle is similar. Strong displays of force can contribute to persuasion as well as deterrence. Tyrants traditionally treat conciliatory actions in response to egregious behavior with contempt: Hitler interpreted Chamberlain's appeasement over Czechoslovakia at Munich as weakness, America's cruise missile retaliation for an Iraqi attempt on former President Bush's life during his 1993 visit to Kuwait did not discourage Baghdad from dispatching army units right up to the border of the oil-rich kingdom in 1994. To resist the Iraqi aggression, Washington had to deploy American troops to Kuwait.

Showing the flag aggressively should not be perceived as an end in itself. Or the target may call the showman's bluff. During the 1962 Cuban missile crisis, Washington demonstrated enough political resolve and military power that Moscow backed down and withdrew its missile batteries from Cuban soil. This standoff became a classic case of a superpower using force to prevent a fundamental change in the balance of power in a vital region.

The exercise of power must not be undercut by ill-advised concessions. For instance, in May 1998 the Clinton administration prompted NATO to display its air power close to Serbia's borders to persuade Milosevic to curb his forces in the province of Kosovo. But the Clinton administration then offered to lift the recently imposed investment bans on Serbia, hoping to facilitate U.S. special envoy Richard Holbrooke's peace negotiations with Belgrade. Subsequent American and NATO policy failed to make up for the misstep, and the situation worsened as special Serb police and army units committed a wave of well-publicized atrocities against Kosovo Albanians during the succeeding five months.

During the Soviet era, deterrence was a mainstay of U.S. policy toward Moscow's nuclear threat. In the post–cold war period, deterrence may also dissuade rogue regimes from spreading biological agents or launching nuclear-armed missiles. But if rogue players persist in deadly actions, then a preemptive strike or counterassault may be in order. Iraq, as an illustration, ignored the U.N. Security Council ultimatum in November 1990 to withdraw from Kuwait during the course of the American-led military buildup in Saudi Arabia and the Persian Gulf. Conflict became the only effective option. Hostilities broke out weeks later as coalition forces counterattacked to drive the Iraqis from Kuwait.

The 1980s witnessed more-accomplished uses of military power for diplomatic motives. In a dramatic exercise, Ronald Reagan ordered the invasion and temporary occupation of Grenada in October 1983. During the two preceding years, Washington had looked with deepening concern at the hundreds of Cuban soldiers who were working on Grenadan construction projects, especially the airport. It soon became apparent that the airport's expansion was intended for military use, not tourism as was officially announced. Reagan's hand was forced when a radical Marxist Soviet-Cuban putsch endangered several hundred American medical students studying on the small Caribbean island, alarming Barbados, Antigua, Dominica, and other tiny states of the region. The Organization of Eastern Caribbean States (OECS) urged the United States to bring order to Grenada and restore democratic government.

A series of reports from Grenada heightened the Reagan administration's fears for the safety of the medical students. Those anxieties deepened when the Grenadan government imposed brutal martial law to suppress legitimate opposition and closed the airport to international landings. After an urgent public appeal from the OECS for U.S. military intervention, the ensuing air and sea invasion encountered some stiff but isolated resistance from the twenty-five hundred Cuban and Grenadan troops. But it soon rescued the students without their suffering any fatalities, repatriated the Cuban contingent, and restored American credibility worldwide. The large-scale military deployment raised American standing after the decline it had suffered with the loss of 241 U.S. Marines in a terrorist bombing in Beirut, followed by the precipitous American departure from Lebanon. The rippling effect of Reagan's projection of power in the Caribbean also had an immediate and proximate reaction. Suriname, located not far from Grenada, reversed its political course and expelled a large Cuban garrison in the wake of the U.S. assault.

President Reagan also struck at Colonel Muammar Qaddafi in retribution for a series of state-sponsored terrorist incidents occurring over several years that culminated in the bombing of a West German discotheque in which two U.S. servicemen died. Long frustrated by being unable to build a coalition among European allies that would impose effective sanctions, the United States retaliated days later with air strikes. Bombs hit Qaddafi's residence and military installations, nearly killing the Libyan dictator. After the bombardment, Libya appeared politically subdued, and some believed that it had been deterred from future terrorism. That judgment was only partially correct; during the balance of the 1980s Qaddafi used violence but sought to disguise his hand in it.[13] For its part, the United States incurred world opprobrium when the U.N. General Assembly passed a resolution condemning the American raid on Libya.

Fighting subversion can invite terrorist reprisals. Reagan's air strikes on Libya probably resulted in the downing of Pan American flight 103 over Lockerbie, Scotland, in December 1988, which killed 259 people aboard the jumbo jet and 11 others on the ground. Evidence pointed to two Libyan agents as having placed the bomb aboard the U.S.-bound flight. The Bush administration responded by getting U.N. sanctions against Libya and insisting that Qaddafi surrender the two suspects for trial either in the United States or in Scotland. To date, Qaddafi has refused to comply but seems open to holding the trial in an unnamed third country.

As the Libyan case demonstrates, counterterrorism—whether punishment or preemptive assaults—can breed a cycle of violence for which the American people must be prepared. A chain reaction of terrorism has already unfolded in the wake of the bombings of the U.S. embassies in Kenya and Tanzania on August 7, 1998. If the future reflects the past, terrorists will certainly avenge President Clinton's firing of cruise missiles at a pharmaceutical plant suspected of producing nerve gas in Sudan and at the paramilitary training camps in Afghanistan. Neither the administration's unconvincing one-shot, remote-control counterattacks nor its bank pincers on the financial assets of Osama bin Laden will win the "war on terrorism." It will take a determined and sustained campaign. A riskless, terrorist-free world is simply beyond realistic attainment, just as is a crime-free society. But a hollow reaction will invite evermore subversion and casualties.

History teaches that a massive application of power is sometimes the only method to deal with a rogue. For example, General Manuel Noriega's corrupt military dictatorship in Panama had bedeviled U.S. drug interdiction efforts for years. Grand juries in Tampa and Miami indicted Noriega for drug trafficking and racketeering in February 1988. Washington's economic sanctions failed to change Noriega's behavior. No opposition movement existed that was capable of wresting power from him, for he enjoyed the backing of the Panama Defense Forces. He put down an attempted coup in March and spurned offers of amnesty in return for going into exile.

America's initial reluctance to employ military force only steeled Noriega's determination to holdout against U.S. economic pressure. His fraudulent claim to reelection in May 1989 deepened skepticism in Bush administration circles that Noriega could be deposed by internal opponents. Panamanian military thugs had also assaulted and killed two American servicemen and attacked members of their families stationed in the Canal Zone. Believing that Noriega's presence endangered the smooth transfer of the canal to Panamanian authority, Bush opted for military intervention. In December 1989 a U.S. airborne invasion—the largest deployed since the Vietnam War—dismantled the PDF, captured Noriega, transported him to a Miami jail to await federal trial and eventual conviction, and restored democracy to Panama.

Finally, Bush led the largest military coalition since World War II to expel Iraq from Kuwait in 1990. He mobilized a 500,000-strong U.S.-led force, convinced a reluctant Congress to back a war against Baghdad, and organized a thirty-nation coalition, many of them Arab countries, to repulse Iraq. His achievement represented a post–cold war highwatermark in U.S. leadership resolved to back American diplomacy with real power.

The Grenada, Panama, and Iraq expeditionary operations shared salient similarities despite their geographic and political differences. Each concentrated massive martial force for limited and achievable strategic objectives. Each succeeded in periods measured in months rather than years. Each saw an American president reach out for international support but fail to win universal consensus. Each witnessed a determined Washington push ahead in the face of domestic and foreign opposition. Each thus represents a milestone in the deployment of forceful measures for national purposes. Reagan and Bush relished foreign affairs. Clinton shirks them. Their records reflect their emphases.

Clinton's Hesitations and Consequences

The Clinton administration's reluctance to employ military power to back its diplomacy is traceable to its first months in office when it was confronted by a series of crises around the globe. The Clintonian "nation-building" designs abruptly crashed on the rocks of political reality in the face of Somalia's chaos and resentment. After the death of eighteen U.S. Army Rangers in Mogadishu during early October 1993 when they sought to capture a local warlord, the Clintonian response to other foreign policy dilemmas grew overcautious, hesitant, and vacillating. The Clinton administration also shifted responsibility to the United Nations in the wake of the Somali debacle. Washington brashly honed this blame-shifting technique to perfection in the course of the Balkan war.

The Somali crisis, and adverse public reaction to it, continued to exert a profound influence on President Clinton. He hesitated far too long in exercising leadership in the Bosnia conflict, after repeated European and U.N. failures to come to grips with the human tragedy. Unfortunately, the Clinton administration adopted the vacillation of the Bush presidency in the Balkans, which should have adopted an assertive policy earlier in the conflict, when it would have been easier to intervene and stop the carnage. Clinton shrank from halting the slaughter until mid-1995, even though as a presidential candidate in 1992 he had declared his opposition to the continuing bloodshed. Meanwhile, the conflict took 200,000 lives.

His administration also tarried overlong in setting things right in Haiti, suffering first a humiliation when Haitian thugs forced the retreat of the USS *Harlan County* and then turning to economic sanctions that worsened the already hard life of ordinary Haitians. Thousands fled harsh conditions for the United States in unseaworthy craft, increasing domestic pressure on the president to resolve the crisis. President Clinton's resoluteness was in short supply for more than a year against the Haitian generals, as Washington's hand-wringing convinced Haiti's military regime that it had little to fear from the Clinton administration, already politically paralyzed by the Somalia crisis. It was not until the force-averse Clinton White House finally gave the green light to an airborne invasion of the Caribbean island in September 1994 that the generals caved in to American demands.

Meanwhile, another human tragedy was unfolding in Central Africa. Washington not only ducked involving U.S. troops in Rwanda to halt the murder of half a million Tutsis by their Hutu countrymen in 1994 but also blocked the United Nations from sending five thousand African troops to forestall mass murder. To Washington's credit, in 1996 Secretary of State Warren Christopher launched the formation of an African crisis response initiative, which set up a regional peacekeeping force to avert or mitigate Rwandan-type bloodbaths. But the perception of irresoluteness gained widespread currency in many capitals when the United States abruptly withdrew from Somalia, hesitated on the Haitian problem, and feebly dithered in the face of the widespread carnage in Bosnia.

A far greater strategic blunder resulted from the Clinton foreign policy team's handling of the North Korean nuclear crisis early in its first administration. North Korea tested the new administration with a script that later would be copied by Iraq and Serbia, projecting implacability interspersed with pragmatism, which led the United States to a settlement that could not be enforced. In the face of sweeping economic and political changes that doomed communism to the historical dustbin, the Democratic People's Republic of Korea (DPRK) stayed wedded to its 1950s Stalinist system. The three-year Korean War ended in 1953, but North Korea's hostile posture toward its southern sister state required stationing thirty-seven thousand U.S. troops on the demilitarized zone (DMZ). The highly charged tension on the DMZ keeps American forces on a battlefield alert. Isolated and impoverished, the DPRK poses two menacing challenges to the United States. First, it continues to maintain a state of war along the world's most fortified border, which separates it from South Korea.

Second, in the late 1980s there were ominous signs that North Korea had embarked on the nuclear weapons path. For decades the DPRK had operated a small nuclear reactor at Yongbyon. But international concern deepened when it became known that the dilapidated cold war relic had been updated with a reprocessing facility that enabled it to develop nuclear warheads. Manufacturing weapons-grade plutonium constituted a violation of the nonproliferation treaty (NPT), which Pyongyang had signed in 1985, although it failed to permit the International Atomic Energy Agency (IAEA) to conduct the mandatory inspections. In late 1992 satellite images confirmed that North Korea was cheating on the NPT. For the next eighteen months, Pyongyang blustered, bluffed, and backed the Clinton administration into an unenforceable agreement that rewarded its bad behavior.[14]

War seemed imminent to Washington during the spring of 1994. Kim Il Sung's despotic regime stonewalled IAEA inspectors, stepped up its bellicose rhetoric toward the South, and moved to replace the spent fuel rods in its reactor, enabling it to harvest enough plutonium for several nuclear warheads. With commensurate skill, Kim alternated conciliatory gestures with tough talk. (The elder Kim's unexpected death in July 1994 presented only a temporary setback to negotiations.) Meanwhile, Washington ruled out an offensive operation, believing that an air strike against underground nuclear facilities offered little prospect for success and might scatter radioactive materials over wide regions of China, Japan, and South Korea, plus more distant countries. Unable to respond with firmness to Pyongyang's development of forbidden weapons, Washington negotiated.

Thus on October 21, 1994, representatives from the United States and North Korea signed the Agreed Framework in Geneva. This intricate agreement called for the crisis to be resolved in phases. Briefly, Pyongyang promised to halt construction of two large Soviet-designed reactors, suspend refueling its out-of-date graphite reactor, and hold its spent fuel rods in cooling ponds for IAEA inspection. In return, the United States and its Japanese and South Korean partners agreed to begin building one and then later another light water nuclear reactor at a cost of $4 billion each. To tide North Koreans over until the new reactors came on line, the Clinton administration agreed to supply fuel oil, reaching a level of 500,000 metric tons a year, for the generation of electrical power. Finally, this agreement stipulated a resumption of North-South talks and the establishment of liaison offices in Washington and Pyongyang, neither of which has yet taken place. Since the signing of the agreement, North Korea has been the top recipient of U.S. foreign assistance in Asia, receiving more than $200 million in foodstuffs to relieve starvation and $100 million in heavy fuel oil.

Hailed by the Clinton administration as a creative response to conflict resolution and North Korean nuclear dreams, the agreement encountered well-founded skepticism in Congress and elsewhere. Setting a dangerous international precedent—giving into blackmail from a declared terrorist state—the agreement substituted deal making for a viable prescription and signaled a readiness to compromise fundamental principles when faced with a bellicose rogue state. The ramifications were global. The Agreed Framework negotiations furnished Iraq and Serbia with a playbook on how to handle American insistence: Make the best deal possible and then carry on as before the agreement. Despite subsequent U.S. efforts to engage the DPRK, it continued subversion against the South and was hostile toward its external benefactors whose food shipments saved thousands of North Korean lives. Since the signing four years ago, alarms have sounded about whether the newly installed Kim Jong Il regime was adhering to the denuclearizing terms of the agreement.

Two events in North Korea during 1998 attested to the validity of those alarms and dealt a blow to the Clinton administration's confidence in Pyongyang. A U.S. satellite revealed images of a large underground complex being constructed near the North Korean nuclear center. Like Iran, the DPRK is believed to be building laboratories and workshops beneath the earth's surface to conceal weapons and missile development and testing. U.S. intelligence officials were amazed at the subterranean facilities' near concealment and their enormous size, which surpass the hidden constructions of Libya, Iraq, and even the Soviet Union in sheer magnitude. Since Pyongyang refused external inspection, speculation centered on the purpose of the complexes for nuclear or missile development.

The second event, a month later, was the test-firing of a long-range North Korean missile. U.S. Navy ships and electronic eavesdropping devices tracked the launch of a multistaged Taepo Dong-1 missile that crossed over northern Japan. Debris from the third stage of the rocket reached nearly four thousand miles into the Pacific. That a North Korean solid-fuel rocket could travel between two and three thousand miles alarmed U.S. military and intelligence officials whose earlier estimates reckoned North Korean capabilities at around a thousand miles. Pyongyang proclaimed that the purpose of the missile was to launch a satellite into orbit. But since a weapon could be substituted for the rocket's satellite payload, fears about the DPRK's growing technological reach were not alleviated.

North Korea's warlike initiatives jeopardized the Clinton administration's arms control agreement with Pyongyang. Critics charged that the Agreed Framework had allowed North Korea the time to become better equipped to do serious damage to U.S. interests in Asia and, perhaps, American lives within the continental United States. Like Iraq, Libya, and other terrorist countries, the DPRK's agenda is inimical to the United States. By accepting North Korea's declarations at face value, the Clinton administration left itself open to charges of gross political naiveté at best and dereliction of duty at worst.

The Clinton national security apparatus should have resisted such a highly leveraged bailout package with a terrorist state. A resolute policy of deterrence would have avoided the risky agreement, which compounded the region's nuclear problems and debilitated antiproliferation efforts with Iraq and Iran. While gaining stiff sanctions against Pyongyang from China and others would have been difficult, the United States could have urged the U.N. Security Council to authorize U.N. member states to intercept exports of the DPRK's nuclear and rocket equipment. Washington and its allies have often had reliable intelligence on North Korean arms shipments but lacked the legal authority to seize them on the high seas.

When in 1998 Japan temporarily balked at continued construction payments, the Clinton White House could have pressed for a renegotiation of the agreement, with the substitution of fossil-fueled plants (coal, oil, gas-fired) to generate nonnuclear electricity. Such a change in course would have lessened tension and better met the energy needs of North Korea without producing electrical overcapacity or heightening nuclear fears. Because the administration still lacks information on how much plutonium was processed in 1994, the agreement should be amended to insist on inspection of all suspected nuclear weapons activities and on the verification of compliance. It seems unlikely, however, that North Korea will relinquish its nuclear bargaining chip for oil and two improved reactors.

In the immediate future, Washington should strengthen the American-Japanese–South Korean defense triangle by stepping up coordination and by pledging to deploy an antimissile defense system early in the next century that could blunt the effectiveness of the North's threats. At a minimum, the United States must robustly deter newly emerging nuclear states, as it did with the Soviet Union in the cold war. The proliferation of nonconventionally armed missiles in the arsenals of rogue states may require a policy of assured destruction of the military capabilities of states developing such weapons. Or it may demand a preemptive strike, as in Israel's bombing of Iraq's Osirak nuclear facility in 1981. Additionally, the United States must construct a reliable national antimissile defense. Research, development, and deployment of a boost-phase interception capability is ultimately the only effective counterweapon against an attack launched from rogue states. An antimissile system—whether by rockets, lasers, or yet-undetermined measures—that promises to explode aggressor missiles over the launcher's homeland will deter their being fired at us.

Low points in American determination and leadership, such as the North Korean negotiations, did not go unnoticed. U.S. reactions encouraged Iraq's recalcitrance in its dealings with U.N. arms inspectors, accounted for North Korea's later face-off with Washington over demands to open its underground facilities to inspection (while demanding $500 million to discontinue missile exports), and bolstered Serbia's reluctance, in the face of U.S.-led NATO efforts, to halt the bloodshed first in Bosnia and then in Kosovo. A high-ranking Chinese military officer, Lieutenant General Xiong Guangkai, deputy chief of China's general staff, reportedly declared in 1995, in response to an American's unofficial warnings that Washington might react militarily to a Beijing attack on Taiwan, "No, you won't. We've watched you in Somalia, Haiti, Bosnia, and you don't have the will."[15]

U.S. hesitancy faced a direct challenge in the Middle East. By mid-1997, Baghdad started a calculated game of cat and mouse to block U.N. Special Commission (UNSCOM) weapons inspectors. The United States, backed only by Britain, tried to obtain a ban on Iraqi international travel from the Security Council. Perceiving American policy as vacillating, France, China, and Russia abstained. Washington's poor showing further emboldened Iraq. Saddam sealed off his country from the UNSCOM teams in November 1997, thereby throwing down a defiant gauntlet to Washington and the United Nations but blaming Washington more than the United Nations for being unfair to Iraq. Authorized by the Security Council, the United States deployed a massive air and sea buildup in the Persian Gulf.

The war clouds that gathered during early 1998 cleared even more suddenly than they had formed, but the triumphant sun shone afterwards on Iraq, not the United States. At the height of the crisis in February, the administration undermined the purpose of a large show of force arrayed against Iraq by plaintively and repeatedly offering "carrots" to Saddam to induce him to permit the U.N. arms inspectors to return. A resumption of the inspections, it was promised, would result in more food shipments and a deescalation of the naval and air buildup.

When the White House withdrew one of the three aircraft carriers in the gulf for a planned refitting rotation, it conveyed a lack of warlike implacability to Saddam. At the apex of the tension, the United States went along with a Security Council move to allow Iraq to double the amount of oil sold under the U.N.-imposed sanctions. Before Kofi Annan ventured to Baghdad for eleventh-hour talks to resolve the crisis, Secretary of State Madeleine Albright had gone to New York City to meet with the United Nations secretary-general and laid out the administration agenda on how to modify the sanctions regime. All these diplomatic signals drained the calculated menace from the administration's naval deployment.

Not surprisingly, Annan succeeded in Baghdad, for Saddam had been led to believe that his grudging cooperation would fulfill the demands for Iraqi compliance. He did agree to "cooperate fully with the U.N. Special Commission and the International Atomic Energy Agency" and to grant them "unconditional and unrestricted access" to sites in Iraq. Baghdad opened previously closed presidential sites to U.N. nuclear, chemical, and biological inspections, albeit with diplomats present. Most experts concluded that the Iraqis had long since removed incriminating evidence. The tension dissipated.

The Iraqi dictator, however, clearly emerged as the winner of the crisis. He achieved several objectives in his political and psychological relationship with the United States and the United Nations. The disagreements over the line to take toward Iraq had split the five permanent members of the Security Council in the run-up to the February showdown when Russia, China, and France stood apart from U.S. policy. Saddam also shifted the international focus from the search for suspected weapons sites to the need to lift the sanctions. Iraq gained a measure of international, including some American, sympathy for its poor, whose plight has been worsened by sanctions. Finally, Saddam, long regarded as a rogue figure, raised his stature by mediating as an equal with the secretary-general, particularly in the Arab world, where many regarded him as a hero for standing up to the United States.

The February standoff served as a dress rehearsal for a similar performance later in 1998. At the end of summer, Iraq again suspended the UNSCOM inspections, and Scott Ritter resigned as the chief of its Concealment Investigations Unit, charging Secretary of State Albright with placing constraints on the inspections. Three months passed before Washington responded. Then, for the fifth time since the gulf war, the Clinton security team dispatched naval and air force units to Iraqi waters and prepared to attack. At almost the last possible minute, the president halted the air assault on Iraqi targets, declaring that Baghdad had once more agreed to cooperate with the U.N. inspectors. Again, UNSCOM returned, and, again, Iraq denied access to some sites requested by the inspectors. It appeared that Saddam Hussein had moved Washington back to square one.

Then, in mid-December, fourteen hours before the scheduled vote on impeachment of the president in the House of Representatives, Clinton unleashed a seventy-hour U.S. and British aerial bombardment against Iraq in what was dubbed as a "containment-plus" policy of sanctions and military actions. Postmortems on Operation Desert Fox were mixed. The Pentagon acknowledged that some four hundred cruise missiles and 650 air sorties hit at least 85 percent of their targets, with 74 percent of the 111 key installations receiving significant damage. But what was doubtful was whether the bombed facilities still housed the suspected weapons. Over the past decade, Baghdad has become a master of concealment, continually hiding and moving production plants, armaments and troops to keep them unobserved by UNSCOM. Most analysts, including some in the Pentagon, concluded that a more intense and sustained campaign was required to harm the regime. Days after the air strikes, Iraqi surface-to-air batteries began firing missiles at U.S. and British planes enforcing the "no-fly" zones to demonstrate at least a symbolic resolve to defend Iraq's sovereignty. Saddam Hussein's anti-aircraft fire and Iraqi violations of the no-fly corridors also signaled a new chapter in his thrust-and-parry strategy in dealing with the United States.

Beyond a military strike, which can be temporarily useful to degrade an immediate threat, the administration's long-range strategy on how to deal with Saddam Hussein remained unclear. It was as if power was applied for the political moment alone without a diplomatic endgame, for no coordination took place between the bombers and clandestine coup makers. Moreover, Washington, almost immediately after the pre-Christmas bombing, began to scale down the U.S. military and naval presence in the Persian Gulf. Hopes that the four days of air strikes might weaken Saddam Hussein's security apparatus soon evaporated, leaving little prospect for an internal coup to remove the Iraqi leader. Some feel that the bombing decision may have represented a politically expedient maneuver rather than a strategic call.

Overt and Covert Operations to Oust a Rogue Regime

If the goal of economic sanctions and demonstrations of force is simply to change a targeted regime's behavior, then the objective of supporting opposition movements is to sweep away the regime itself. As such, interventionist steps constitute vigorous measures short of war to advance U.S. interests. They can embrace open and secret operations. They can provide limited financial backing and technical assistance to opposition parties pitted against entrenched regimes. Or they can fuel armed struggle. The National Endowment for Democracy (NED), since is inception in 1983, has promoted democracy overtly in a host of countries worldwide. Funded by Congress with annual appropriations, the NED openly channels monies to prodemocracy groups to foster free elections, individual and minority rights, open media communications, and the rule of law. The National Democratic Institute and the International Republican Institute, both loosely affiliated with the two major political parties, likewise promote democratic measures abroad.

But a different order of magnitude of aid is required for underground movements waging an armed insurgency. Sponsoring these types of regime opponents can mean supplying military training, sophisticated weapons, and intelligence information. Backing insurgent operations can also mean sending training missions into hostile territory and prescribing no-fly zones, and perhaps even "no-drive" zones to keep a targeted regime from mounting armored counteroffensives on liberated areas within its own territory. Funds can also be set aside for the dissemination of information and radio broadcasts to rally government opponents. The most extreme form of covert operation involves sending in U.S. ground forces. However, inserting American troops, not training teams, into a prolonged antiregime insurgency is usually bad policy. It Americanizes a conflict, causing a spate of troubles, including a nationalistic counterreaction from the inhabitants of the besieged country and U.S. domestic opposition to the venture, as demonstrated by the Vietnam War.

Rebel movements employ violence and endanger lives and property to destabilize a foreign government. Short of declared war, nuclear conflict, or a gulf war–style invasion, insurgent operations or inside-the-palace coups represent a most potent foreign policy instrument. A more serious threat to rogue leaders than cruise missile strikes or aerial bombardments, which seldom endanger the survival of a dictatorial regime because of the difficulty in hitting its leader, they can tap into deep-seated grievances, give model and focus to inchoate opposition efforts, offer inducements to followers, and sometimes build political momentum.

At the same time, they possess many drawbacks for Washington. Covert operations seldom remain covert for long. Once exposed to media coverage and political censure, they can become election liabilities, for democratic nations are understandably unsuited for secret wars. Underground political movements are also subject to penetration and subversion. The intrigue, factional struggles, political assassinations, and internecine quarrels that form part of most insurgent movements are particularly troubling to free societies.

U.S. covert, or secret, operations have been legendary exploits to some and a disreputable chapter in America's external relations to others. The crucible of secret wars, clandestine military operations, and assistance to underground resistance movements lies in the World War II experience, during which espionage complemented and reinforced more traditional battlefield maneuvers. As such, it was an acceptable form of combat against hostile states during a declared war.

Since the end of World War II, however, covert operations have assumed a significant role in the pursuit of U.S. foreign policy objectives short of open conflict. Because secret operations were directed against foreign governments in the absence of a declared war, they have become controversial within the United States as well as in the international community. Critics paint the U.S. role in the destabilization of the Mossadegh regime in Iran during 1953, the Arbenz government in Guatemala in 1954, and Chile's Allende government in 1973 as dark episodes in America's foreign affairs. To critics, the United States was wrong to overthrow those populist governments because they represented the poor and downtrodden against the moneyed classes and U.S. corporate interests. The critics also judged such covert operations as illegal under international law. The realists, however, viewed the subversion of anti-American leaders as legitimate because their regimes endangered U.S. strategic interests, were aligned with Moscow, and harmed legitimate American commercial enterprises.

The "ends justifying the means" controversy still confronts policymakers whenever they plan to eliminate an anti-American regime. In some cases, such as Iraq, where the people suffer from unchecked despotism, the argument against change by externally backed destabilization sounds overly legalistic, fainthearted, and it wrongly validates an unjust tyrant's claim to political authority.

It was the war in Southeast Asia, however, that cast a shadow on all clandestine operations. That conflict, virtually a full-scale war, incorporated numerous covert actions that were a major part of the U.S. counterinsurgency campaign. Secret warfare became even more unpopular among sections of American society with, first, Reagan's contra war against the Nicaraguan Sandinistas and then his subordinates' opening back-channel relations with Iran for secret weapons sales to fund the contras in violation of congressional statutes. Reagan's Central American policy, which strained relations with Latin American countries and stirred opposition in Congress and within the United States, was predicated on denying the Soviet Union another base, in addition to Cuba, in this hemisphere. The contras' guerrilla war may have generated domestic turmoil, but it thwarted the formation of a militant Marxist government in Nicaragua.

In Afghanistan, Reagan aided the anticommunist mujahideen in repelling the Soviet Union, which had launched an invasion in 1979. American arms, particularly the Stinger heat-seeking, shoulder-fired missile, were credited with turning the tide against the Soviet army's occupation. Even this textbook case, however, has incurred second thoughts. Critics of the Reagan doctrine now charge that American arms and martial instruction contributed to the political fragmentation of Afghan society and the rise of the Taliban, the extreme Muslim sect that controls most of country. But reality is much more complex in Afghanistan, where ancient tribal cleavages divide the mountainous people and the Soviets relied on local puppets to retain control. In short, Afghanistan was a subdivided country well before the Americans aided the resistance.

Proponents of covert operations argue that clandestine investments and toughness yield positive results for American policy when other courses of action are not an option. The Soviet Union lost conflicts in its backyard and ours because of Reagan-initiated measures short of war.

Those defeats, particularly in Afghanistan, unsettled Soviet leadership and society, paving the way for the rise of Gorbachev and the dissolution of the USSR. With the United States confronting a despot in Iraq, where sanctions and shows of force have yielded limited results, it is necessary to reconsider supporting opposition elements so as to remove a ruthless leader before he acquires superweapons and long-range missiles. The historical record reminds us, of course, that clandestine actions seldom remain hidden from public scrutiny and thus should be in accord with international norms.

Iraq and Iran

Despite the high stakes, Washington has demonstrated a curious irresoluteness toward Iraqi bad behavior for much of this decade. Yet Iraq poses serious threats to the Persian Gulf littoral, where 65 percent of the world's oil reserves are located, and American allies, particularly Israel.

The Bush and Clinton administrations failed to sustain the one major threat that had—and still has—the potential to topple Saddam: an internal opposition. Two distinct elements—an army coup or a popular revolt—seemed likely to overthrow the regime after the Iraqi defeat in early 1991, which would have spared the United States great expense and exertion. Fearing a protracted military campaign, abandonment by Arab allies, or even a Vietnam-type quagmire in Iraq, Bush suspended the war without displacing Saddam Hussein. Instead, he called on the Iraqis to overthrow their discredited leader. When they did revolt in the southern Shiite-dominated region, however, he did nothing to help them on the grounds that the country might fragment, leaving Iran, Turkey, and Saudi Arabia to grab territory. Like many political experts, Bush believed that the heads of defeated governments nearly always fall from power as a consequence of national humiliations. But stern dictators can repeal the laws of Western political scientists with little effort.

Another promising opportunity to subvert Saddam Hussein's authority was consigned by the Clinton administration to a fate similar to that of Bush's postwar rebels. Iraqi dissidents from the Kurdish and Shiite communities united to form an umbrella organization, known in the West as the Iraqi National Congress (INC), at a meeting in Vienna in mid-1992. Soon afterward, the INC set about establishing an embryonic insurgent state in northern Iraq, which lay within the no-fly zone established by the United Nations. It was protected by lightly armed American infantry under U.S. Operation Provide Comfort. The INC set up a network of agents to disseminate propaganda, gather intelligence, and carry out political organizing in this insurgent state. Under Bush, the Central Intelligence Agency supplied the funding for these limited INC activities.

The new Clinton government, however, changed U.S. policy toward Iraq in hopes of resolving differences with Baghdad. In January 1993, the president-elect declared that normal relations with Iraq could be achieved not by Saddam's removal but by a behavioral alteration on the part of the Iraqi leader. Clinton argued, "If he [Saddam Hussein] wants a different relationship with the United States and the United Nations, all he has to do is change his behavior."[16] As president, Clinton reduced financial aid to covert actions as part of his revised approach. Furthermore, the new president responded limply to the revelation that Iraq had plotted to assassinate former President Bush in the course of a private tour of Kuwait in 1993. When Baghdad moved troops up to the Kuwaiti border in 1994, the United States rushed reinforcements to Kuwait but administered no punishment to Iraq. These hollow responses only encouraged Saddam's bad behavior.

The Clinton administration then threw away one of the best means to rid Iraq of Saddam by reining in the INC, which in late 1994 and early 1995 was poised to expand its operating area in northern Iraq, where autonomous Kurdish enclaves had been established at the end of the gulf war. This no-fly zone had taken on aspects of a burgeoning insurgent state called Kurdistan and declared a U.N. "safe haven." But the United States proved unwilling or unable to head off factionalism among the Kurds, which once more split them apart and contributed to the debacle that took place in late summer 1996. One of the factions entered into an expedient alliance with Baghdad, enabling its armed columns to move northward with near impunity.

When Iraqi tanks rolled into the Kurdish enclave, the United States stood aside. Saddam's troops extirpated the INC networks, destroyed the resistance's base, and shot scores of INC adherents. Several days afterward, the administration launched cruise missiles against military targets hundreds of miles away and expanded the no-fly zone in the south, not the north. Those pinpricks encouraged bolder actions against U.N. arms inspectors and badly damaged American credibility in northern Iraq and elsewhere. The anti-Saddam resistance suffered a near fatal blow, and Washington gained the reputation of an untrustworthy friend.

Long critical of Secretary of State Albright's assurances that Saddam would be kept "in his box," Capitol Hill introduced and passed a bipartisan bill—the Iraq Liberation Act of 1998—before the midterm elections. That bill embodied four major components: (1) It called for a policy that would remove the Saddam Hussein regime. (2) It authorized the president to expend funds for a Radio Free Iraq and military aid to the Iraq opposition forces. (3) It renewed congressional calls for an international tribunal to try Saddam and other Iraqi officials as war criminals. (4) Looking to a post-Saddam Iraq and some of the issues of rebuilding a shattered society, it authorized $97 million in equipment and arms from U.S. military stocks and gave the president ninety days to designate Iraqi opposition groups for the assistance. Clinton signed the bill and rhetorically, at least, turned to its provisions to deal with Saddam Hussein.

In September 1998 Paul Wolfowitz, undersecretary of defense in the Bush administration, advanced a proposal before the U.S. House of Representatives' National Security Committee to establish a "liberated zone" in southern Iraq. That corner had witnessed pitted resistance to Baghdad from the predominantly Shiite population following the gulf war. Saddam's soldiers ruthlessly crushed the rebellion and imposed a reign of terror over the inhabitants in the village marshes, which continued to harbor separatist sentiments. The Baghdad government, made up mainly of the minority Sunni Muslims, repressed other communities with elements of religious as well as political intolerance. Other voices called for a protectorate in the north among the Kurds or encouraged Iraqi generals to overthrow their chief.

The Wolfowitz plan envisioned an insurgent state that would attract disaffected army units, rally political opposition, and in time lead to "the unraveling of the regime." The United States would at first provide defense for this protectorate, which in time could assume a greater degree of its own defense. In Wolfowitz's script, Baghdad's frozen assets, valued at $1.6 billion, would gradually flow to the free Iraq zone. The provisional government of a future free Iraq would enjoy international recognition, protection, and control of the country's largest oil field. Most ingeniously, a viable pocket of resistance would compel French, Russian, and other backers of Saddam Hussein to recalculate their support because the hoped-for parallel entity would have the power to grant lucrative commercial and petroleum opportunities to its friends. No commercially aspiring foreign capital wants to burn bridges to lucrative deals with a post-Saddam Iraq.

Fomenting a successful rebellion against the ruthless Saddam Hussein is a daunting challenge. There are many ways that such formidable plans can go wrong. U.S. policy will no doubt suffer setbacks and embarrassments. Opposition movements historically spend resources fighting among themselves, and conspiratorial political organizations lend themselves to penetration by their enemy's agents provocateurs. Underground movements often instigate harebrained operations that in retrospect appear farcical as well as doomed to defeat, such as the Cuban exiles' Bay of Pigs invasion. Arming, training, and financing an insurrection do not guarantee a movement's foregone victory. President Kennedy's assistance to anti-Castro Cubans faltered when he called off air support for their beach landing, ending in disaster for them and making his new administration appear weak to Moscow. Reagan's aid to Angolan opponents of the Marxist government in Luanda brought neither triumph nor peace, for the largely ethnic conflict still smolders in the countryside. It is possible that a growing opposition movement will spur a military coup in Baghdad, but the generals will want to be certain that the Iraqi dictator is doomed before leaving the barracks.

Even if an opposition movement succeeds in dispatching the Iraqi despot, there is no guarantee that his successor will be much of an improvement. There also exists the prospect of a splintered Iraq, torn apart by Kurds and Sunni and Shiite Arabs. Insurrection may result in fragmentation, but Iraq's dissolution may come about no matter how the Saddam regime crumbles. Neighboring states will loathe the dramatic consequences of an anti-Saddam rebellion and may try to control parts of Iraq. Their acquiescence, if not active assistance, is the sine qua non for advancing an insurrectionary enclave in Iraq. Saudi Arabia fears that Iran will gain from unrest in Iraq. The potential creation of another Shia state is anathema to Riyadh and the Gulf states. Turkey is also alarmed by the prospect of a strengthened Kurdish enclave in northern Iraq for the added danger it would pose to Ankara's Kurdish problem. Aside from approval from bordering states, the key variable in underwriting an anti-Saddam movement is credible American commitment. Knowing that Washington is prepared to back a revolt may cause Saddam Hussein to blunder or stiffen the resolve of would-be rebels or both, which might redound to U.S. advantage.

International law also conflicts with foreign-sponsored assaults on national sovereignty. But Iraq's contempt for its own citizens, aggression against neighbors, and willingness to use catastrophic weapons dilute its legal defense in international forums. Washington and its partners can recognize a government in exile to offset some of the complaints. Critics will still charge the United States with aggression. But sober opinion will recognize the danger of an armory of nuclear, biological or chemical weapons in the hands of the murderous Iraqi leader, even if public statements condemn the United States.

Despite the obstacles, overthrowing Saddam Hussein will demonstrate to other rogue dictators the dangers of crossing swords with the international community, led by the United States. The United States will be seen by the world at large as pursuing its policies with as much vigor as its more bloodthirsty adversaries. Most significantly, it represents the only realistic step toward a less threatening and aggressive Iraq. Containment fatigue is well advanced among regional states and some U.S. allies. The present course of action is costly, demoralizing, and, most likely, unsustainable for much longer.

Engineering internal opposition to rogue regimes may also be an operable strategy against other rogue states. After Iranians seized the American embassy in Tehran in 1979, the new and revolutionary Islamic Republic of Iran imposed a theocratic regime led by Ayatollah Khomeini, who deposed the shah, that sought to control every aspect of life in Iran. It declared the United States the "Great Satan" and sponsored terrorism against America and its allies, chiefly Israel. Iran is suspected of having a hand in the bombings against U.S. military installations in Riyadh in November 1995 and Dhahran, Saudi Arabia, in June 1996 as well as substantially funding Hezbollah terrorism against Israel. Since Khomeini's death, Iran's revolutionary ardor has cooled among some elements of the population.

The 1997 election of President Mohammad Khatami, who is perceived as politically moderate, has softened Tehran's anti-American rhetoric to a degree. Iran's recent foreign policy showed signs of pragmatism and openness to improved relations with Washington. But the country's autocratic fundamentalism still grips much of Iranian society. The president's moderation is opposed by extremist clerics, who aim to turn the clock back on modernism and Westernization before they are marginalized by reform. At this juncture, the political direction of Iran hangs in the balance. Official Iranian policy disapproves of direct relations with Washington, which it criticizes for anti-Iranian actions. But the Iranian majority opposes the theocratic strictures imposed by Muslim clerics. The most worrisome current development is the country's designs on acquiring nuclear and biological weapons capabilities and long-range missiles, as evidenced by production and testing of its Shihab missile series.

Washington has reciprocated Islamic-ruled Iran's early hostile acts by freezing Iranian financial assets at the time of the embassy takeover, imposing economic sanctions, blocking construction of an oil pipeline through Iranian territory from the Caspian Sea, and planning a Persian-language radio station in Prague for broadcasts into Iran. Sanctions have little chance of destabilizing the government, although they are nettlesome to the economy and government. With the prospect of a thaw in American-Iranian relations, the Clinton administration in its second term warmed to the hints of better relations emanating from Teheran. But to date Iranian-American interchanges are far short of a genuine rapprochement.

Iran is not considered to have a domestic opposition capable of supplanting the theocratic rearguard at this time, but the overwhelming election and rising popularity of President Khatami affords an opportunity to expand on the desire for change. Whenever possible, Washington should bolster the prochange forces within Iranian elites and society. President Reagan's backing of the Solidarity movement in Poland contributed to the unraveling of that country's communist government. Although Iran does have ethnic vulnerabilities, particularly with its twenty million Azeris, who constitute about a third of Iran's population, this ethnic community shares none of the extreme disaffection with the regime that the Kurds in Iraq have in their regime. Therefore, Washington's best option for government reform is to encourage the forces of change while striving to limit Iran's drive for weapons of mass destruction.

Kosovo and the Balkans

During most of 1998, the gap widened between Clinton's declared goals of halting the mass murder of Kosovo Albanians and forming an effective strategy. Just as the Serbian president earlier brazenly pushed his proxies ahead in Bosnia, so did Milosevic dispatch armed units to murder and intimidate the Albanian population who make up 90 percent of Kosovo and seek independence from Belgrade. Milosevic's reign of terror in Kosovo, an autonomous province of Serbia until 1989, cried out for resolution because of both its cost in human lives and its political disruption of the region. Albanian refugees spilled across borders into Macedonia, Albania, and the still-restive Bosnia, threatening them with political instability and conjuring up fears of a greater Albania among some observers.

With the conflict raging in Bosnia-Herzegovina, the Clinton administration, facing the prospect of a Bosnian Serb triumph over the disintegrating Yugoslav province, looked to bolstering an opposition by equipping, training, and financing Croatian armed forces. With tacit approval of the U.S. Department of State, a private company began to operate in the newly formed Croatia. By at least late 1994, Military Professional Resources Incorporated (MPRI), based in Alexandria, Virginia, had begun instructing Croatian officers in military strategy and tactics. The Croats also acquired massive amounts of modern armaments, including recent-vintage tanks, attack helicopters, fixed-wing aircraft, and automatic rifles. News accounts reported that Germany along with wealthy Croatians abroad funneled at least $1.3 billion into the smuggling of weapons. Moreover, Croatian authorities skimmed weapons from Iranian arms shipments intended for Bosnian Muslims. NATO turned a blind eye to most of this arms traffic.[17]

American assistance, which helped account for the successful Croatian blitzkrieg in the Krajina region, represents the right type of action to counter aggression without involving U.S. or NATO ground forces. The Croatian counterattack smashed the Bosnian Serbs' offensive and dispelled the myth of Serb invincibility, which had lingered since World War II, when Serbian guerrillas tied down the Nazi invasion in prolonged military campaigns. Croatia's rollback of Bosnian Serb advances during mid-1995 was a major reason the Serbs agreed first to a cease-fire and then to meet in Dayton, Ohio, in December to iron out an agreement. NATO's air attacks in early fall and Croatian advances on the ground convinced Milosevic to exert pressure on his Bosnian Serb clients to accept the Dayton settlement.

The specter of another round of genocide in the heart of Europe offered strategic and moral rationale enough for U.S. and NATO to douse the Kosovo fire with a limited form of intervention in late 1998, but it proved incapable of halting interethnic massacres. All the earnest sentiments expressed about a revamped NATO mission in post-Soviet eastern Europe, however, will ring false without the Atlantic alliance stabilizing the Balkans and permanently ending the annihilation of the Kosovars. No peace will come to Kosovo or Bosnia as long as Serbia is ruled by an undemocratic regime. Milosevic's despotic grip is not amenable to electioneering or parliamentary change. Effort to oust him through a parliamentary vote failed when he banned Montenegro's deputies from their seats in the federal parliament. Like Saddam Hussein, it will require an internal force to overthrow him and replace his government with a democratic one.

A comprehensive plan to oust Milosevic, like aid to separatist movements in Iraq, can strengthen ties to potential secessionists. Montenegro, the last remaining state besides Serbia in the former Yugoslavia, seems a likely place to begin. Montenegrins already chafe at Belgrade's economic embargo, political control, and second-class treatment, and Milosevic has campaigned to undo President Milo Djukanovic's reformist administration. Thus, American entreaties to the Djukanovic government will fall on receptive soil. A stronger Montenegro could increase U.S. leverage against Milosevic. Montenegro's departure from the remaining Yugoslav federation would strip away even the superficial legitimacy binding Kosovo to the Serbian-dominated entity and strike at the heart of the rump of Yugoslavia. But the Republika Srpska, the Serbian ministate in the Dayton-created Croat-Bosnian state, will most likely seek to unite with Serbia, thereby undercutting the Dayton multiethnic federation.

Other elements of an anti-Milosevic campaign could include air and missile bombardments of military targets within Serbia, if they would weaken the regime. But the Serbian armed forces, having recently conducted top-echelon purges, may now be a reliable prop to the beleaguered Milosevic dictatorship. Aiding democratic opponents is likely to be a more fruitful policy, including a program of engagement with democratic forces. High-level U.S. and European visitors to Belgrade should demand meetings with opposition politicians. We should insist that nongovernmental organizations and European and American journalists be granted access to Serbia and to independent media, journalists, and academicians. Funds should be made available for Serbian dissidents to travel to the West and to organize domestic activities. Most decisively, assistance should be made available to the Kosovo Liberation Army (KLA).

Owing to Washington's endorsement of autonomy, not independence, for Kosovo, substantial aid and encouragement were withheld from the independence-oriented KLA. This official posture is untenable. Albanians have been radicalized by their persecution. Their onetime goal of autonomy from Belgrade has been superseded by a passion for outright independence. Milosevic's intransigence to any modification of the Kosovo-Serbian relationship makes genuine peace improbable. By resorting to the mass murder, torture, and rape of Albanians, Serbian security forces have sown discord in the region that will not abate for generations. The lessening of the Serbian slaughter resembles an armed truce, not a lasting state of peace. True peace and stability await a regime change in Belgrade.

The United States can arm and resupply proxy movements, as it did the freedom fighters in Afghanistan and Nicaragua. Military advisers can provide training to resistance groups in tactics and strategy as well as sophisticated weapons and equipment. Aid can include financial resources for organizing purposes and humanitarian assistance. Intelligence data should also be furnished to enable friendly elements to defeat their—and our—adversaries. One can only speculate on whether Serbian opposition parties will overcome their disunity to defeat Milosevic's regime. No speculation, however, is needed on how meager organizations like Poland's Solidarity can blossom into democraticizing forces if internationally backed.

In the realm of diplomacy, the United States can put pressure on neighboring states to help post–cold war freedom fighters with across-the-border sanctuaries for training and resupply and grant them diplomatic backing. Washington can also represent the interests of insurgent groups with other powers. This is an ambitious agenda, but without a firm commitment we put ourselves at risk from ruthless rogues.

Conclusion and Recommendations

At the dawn of a new millennium, the United States finds itself entering an era of neither war nor peace. Rather, it confronts an uncertain and increasingly deadly world. We face not one arms race but many, in which weapons of mass destruction have fallen—or are falling—into the most desperate hands. Rogue adversaries covet nuclear, chemical, or biological capabilities to obliterate ancient enemies or to terrorize their way into the circles of the great powers. They are also rapidly acquiring the long-range missiles to deliver awesome destruction to our allies' and our own shores. A congressionally chartered Commission to Assess the Ballistic Missile Threat to the United States under the chairmanship of Donald Rumsfeld concluded in 1998 that Iran and North Korea will be able "to inflict major destruction on the United States" within five years and Iraq within ten. How the United States handles rogue states will be of decisive importance to America's well-being and global primacy. If it is judged timorous in the use of power, it will be open to challenge as its own vulnerability becomes apparent.

Clausewitz, the famous Prussian military theorist, emphasized that war is to be understood as the continuation of politics by other means. Our adoption of severe remedies short of declared conflict must be seen as an extension of diplomatic instruments to realize our strategic goals. Power must be employed to further diplomatic goals.

Sanctions and criminal legal proceedings make up part of our arsenal. These initial steps can build international support for more draconian measures. Offensive military operations and other measures short of war are our best defense for peace and continued security. They represent political warfare, provided, of course, that the United States has the tenacity and wherewithal to complete them once begun.

By backing away from realistic approaches we will demonstrate to our opponents that they can oppose us without cost. Our allies will take note and go their own way. This turn of events will cause still further problems down the road. If the forces of global disorder come to dominate the world scene, the human condition will be degraded, producing fertile soil for still more extreme elements to take root. The alternative to American leadership is growing international anarchy. Unless we restore power, and the credibility it represents, to U.S. diplomacy, we await the dire consequences of our feebleness.

Notes

1. George Shultz, *Turmoil and Triumph: My Years as Secretary of State* (New York: Charles Scribner's Sons, 1993), p. 10.
2. Robert E. Harkavy, "The Pariah State Syndrome," *Orbis: A Journal of World Affairs* 21, no. 3 (fall 1977): 623–28.
3. For more on the sheriff analogy, see Richard Haass, *The Reluctant Sheriff: The United States after the Cold War* (New York: Council on Foreign Relations, 1997), pp. 93–100.
4. Zbigniew Brzezinski, *The Grand Chessboard: American Primacy and its Geostrategic Imperatives* (New York: Basic Books, 1997), p. 214.
5. Shultz, *Turmoil and Triumph*, p. 345.
6. *A Catalog of New U.S. Unilateral Economic Sanctions for Foreign Policy Purposes, 1993–96* (Washington: D.C.: National Association of Manufacturers, 1997), p. 1; Richard N. Haass, editor, *Economic Sanctions and American Diplomacy* (New York: Council of Foreign Relations, 1998), pp. 197–211; Jesse Helms, "What Sanctions Epidemic? U.S. Business' Curious Crusade," *Foreign Affairs* 78, no. 1 (January–February 1999): 2–8.
7. Gary Clyde Hufbauer, Jeffrey J. Schott, and Kimberly Ann Elliott, *Eco-*

nomic Sanctions Reconsidered: History and Current Policy (Washington, D.C.: Institute for International Economics, 1990), p. 7.
8. Gary Clyde Hufbauer, Jeffrey J. Schott, Kimberly Ann Elliott. *Economic Sanctions Reconsidered: Supplemental Case Histories*, 2d ed. (Washington, D.C.: Institute for International Economics, 1990), pp. 285–93.
9. Richard Holbrook, *To End a War* (New York: Random House, 1998), pp. 250, 259.
10. For more on the ICC, see John C. Bolton, "Courting Danger," *National Interest*, no. 54 (winter, 1998/99): 60–71.
11. For more on this argument, see Robert Thompson, *Defeating Communist Insurgency: Experiences from Malaya and Vietnam* (London: Chatto & Windus, 1966), p. 52.
12. Lee Michael Katz, "Money Trail Leads to Terror Networks," *USA Today*, October 1, 1998, p. 1.
13. Bruce Hoffman, *Inside Terrorism* (New York: Columbia University Press, 1998), p. 192.
14. For a detailed treatment of the Clinton administration's negotiations, see Thomas H. Henriksen, *Clinton's Foreign Policy in Somalia, Bosnia, Haiti, and North Korea* (Stanford: Hoover Institution, 1996), pp. 29–38.
15. Barton Gellman, "U.S. and China Nearly Came to Blows in 1996," *Washington Post*, June 21, 1998, p. 1.
16. "Excerpts from an Interview with Clinton after the Air Strikes," *New York Times*, January 14, 1993, p. A8.
17. Uli Schmetzer, "How West Let Croatia Sneak Arms," *Chicago Tribune*, August 20, 1995, p.1; Jack Kelley, "Wellspring of Weapons amid 'Leaky' Embargo," *USA Today*, August 14, 1995, p. 4A.

ESSAYS IN PUBLIC POLICY

Using Power and Diplomacy to Deal with Rogue States Thomas H. Henriksen, 1999

The Congressional Response to Social Security Surpluses, 1935–1994 John F. Cogan, 1998

Hong Kong under Chinese Rule: The First Year David Newman and Alvin Rabushka, 1998

Affirmative Action in Higher Education: A Dilemma of Conflicting Principles John H. Bunzel, 1998

Reengineering College Student Financial Aid Robert Pernell Huff, 1998

India: Asia's Next Tiger? Hilton L. Root, 1998

Some Thoughts on Improving Economic Statistics Michael J. Boskin, 1998

Inflation and Its Discontents Michael J. Boskin, 1997

The Ten Causes of the Reagan Boom: 1982–1997 Martin Anderson, 1997

Political Money: The New Prohibition Annelise Anderson, 1997

Immigration and the Rise and Decline of American Cities Stephen Moore, 1997

Freedom's Fall in Hong Kong Alvin Rabushka, 1997

U.S. Foreign Policy and Intellectual Property Rights in Latin America Edgardo Buscaglia and Clarisa Long, 1997

Nuclear Blackmail: The 1994 U.S.– Democratic People's Republic of Korea Agreed Framework on North Korea's Nuclear Program Victor Gilinsky, 1997

The 1996 House Elections: Reaffirming the Conservative Trend David Brady, John F. Cogan, and Douglas Rivers, 1997

Prospects for Democratic Development in Africa Larry Diamond, 1997

North Korea at a Crossroads Robert A. Scalapino, 1997

Clinton's Foreign Policy in Somalia, Bosnia, Haiti, and North Korea Thomas H. Henriksen, 1996

Culture Wars in America Edward P. Lazear, 1996

North Korean Economic Reform and Political Stability Bruce Bueno de Mesquita and Jongryn Mo, 1996

Taxation and Economic Performance W. Kurt Hauser, 1996

The Democratic Advantage: The Institutional Sources of State Power in International Competition Kenneth A. Schultz and Barry R. Weingast, 1996

Let's Wait for Korea to Decide: An Essay on the Hoover Conference "A New Economic Relationship: The United States and Korea" Jongryn Mo, 1996

Judicial Reform in Latin America: A Framework for National Development Edgardo Buscaglia, Maria Dakolias, and William Ratliff, 1995

Taiwan and the United Nations: Conflict between Domestic Policies and International Objectives Harvey J. Feldman, 1995

China's Economic Revolution and Its Implications for Sino-U.S. Relations Ramon H. Myers, 1995

Has China Lost Its Way? Getting Stuck in Transition Hilton L. Root, 1995

Global Warming: A Boon to Humans and Other Animals Thomas Gale Moore, 1995

Publications in this series address public policy issues or developments of interest to a broad audience including government officials, the media, and scholars. Some recent essays are posted on our website (http://www-hoover.stanford.edu). A complete list of Essays in Public Policy published since 1984 is available on request.

HOOVER INSTITUTION PRESS
Stanford University · Stanford, CA 94305-6010 · (650) 723-3373